ASCENSION GUIDEBOOK

Pleiadian Guides reveal the Four Energy Activations that prepare Earth Beings for Ascension in 2012

THE TECHNOLOGY OF ASCENSION SERIES

Book Two

By

Duane Henkle

Crystal Triangle Publishing
Vancouver, WA

The Ascension Guidebook

Did you ever dream about coming to planet Earth to participate in the greatest spiritual adventure in the history of all humanity?

You did! You can! You are!

Pleiadian Guides reveal Four Energy Activations that prepare Earth Beings for Ascension in 2012

Introduction and editing: Diana Stone
Cover design: Donald Hurd
Illustrations: Richard Chavez and Donald Hurd
Page Composition and book design: Donald Hurd

Other books by Duane Henkle:

The Lightbody Activation Manual
First Edition published February 2003
Second Edition published December 2003
Third Edition published November 2005 by:

Crystal Triangle Publishing
12005 N.W. 14th Avenue
Vancouver, WA 98685
www.dianastone.com

Printed in the United States of America
Library of Congress Control Number: 2006920758

ISBN-13: 978-0-9725745-3-2
ISBN-10: 0-9725745-3-0

Dedication

At the Bridge

It is 2012
As you approach the bridge leading
to the Fifth Dimension
you are asked just one question.
You must answer truthfully.
"Were you more in service to yourself or
were you more in service to others?"

This book is dedicated to light workers everywhere who are in service to others and moving this world ever closer to Ascension.

Table of Contents

Introduction

Introduction

By

Diana Stone

Duane Henkle is one of the high-profile voices in the ascension movement. This book, *The Ascension Guidebook*, is the second in the series: THE TECHNOLOGY OF ASCENSION. His first book, *The Lightbody Activation Manual,* was published in 2003, in collaboration with his sister, Diana Stone.

Heightened awareness of ascension has exploded into the mass consciousness since the publication of the first book. Information about the subject is awash on the Internet. A proliferation of recently published books and articles increasingly includes material about ascension from many points of view. Individuals and groups all over the world are using the Lightbody Activation method described in Book One. (For the convenience of readers, the nine-step Fifth Dimension Lightbody Activation method from that book is reproduced in this volume.)

Harmonic Concordance Day

A significant date in the ascension process was Harmonic Concordance Day observed by people all over the globe on November 8-9, 2003. On that date, which featured a rare Star of David planetary line-up, Pleiadian extraterrestrials once again transmitted information directly to Duane. These were the very same Beings--the name is their preference--that taught Duane the Lightbody Activation method in Hawaii. Readers who are new to this subject are strongly urged to read the first book for the entire background story.

After months of working with clients worldwide after Harmonic Concordance, three activations were added to the original Fifth Dimension Lightbody Activation to become the four activations that are the basis for this present book. The four activations now include the Fifth, Sixth and Seventh Dimensions plus the very critically important 12-strand DNA Activation. These processes are the ones used to construct an ascension vehicle in which one ascends into the Fifth Dimension (this vehicle is not the foreign import kind with four wheels).

The enthusiastic responses from clients to these additions to the original lightbody work made it clear that the Pleiadian Beings once again repeated the successes that have become so obvious from the Fifth Dimension method by itself. The book includes some case studies and testimonials which represent people from all walks of life and varying levels of awareness.

The Lightbody Activation Manual (Book One) described the participation of helpers from the special consciousness of the crystal kingdom. Some readers may be aware of the power of crystals. *The Lightbody Activation Manual* described a method that incorporated the use of specially programmed crystals. The new methods in this book once again utilize specific crystals with detailed instructions and illustrations in how to use them every step of the way to do the four activations by yourself at home. Duane also described in the first book his amazing relationship with power animals that came to him to volunteer their services throughout the ascension period, i.e., Sea Turtle and Dolphin. These remain the two power animals participating in aiding humanity through this time of evolutionary change.

Anyone Can Do It

THE TECHNOLOGY OF ASCENSION SERIES is not exclusively for those individuals who are sophisticated in their knowledge and experience of the ascension process. It is for virtually everybody. The author is aware that this is a paradigm shift that is confusing and unbelievable for many readers. The material in this book was designed by the Pleiadians in order to extend the opportunity of the coming Shift to individuals who have no special knowledge of ascension by providing simple tools. The method combines crystals along with programmed movements in a receiving partner's energy field. By temporarily allowing oneself to ignore the intellectual need for detailed understanding and by just following the precise directions in this book, you will be convinced by the self-evident results.

Most people are aware of the evolutionary process. It is usually thought of only in terms of changes in *physical* forms. However, consciousness also evolves. At whatever level changes occur, the forces of evolution build up energies over long periods of time until they reach critical mass. That is exactly what is happening at the present time. Humanity is headed for a leap in consciousness into another dimension, the Fifth. This is a unique evolutionary step in that the Earth is also preparing to make the change along with us.

The date that is most often given for this event is December 2012. There are multiple sources for this date and this information; the Mayan calendar, the Hopi Indians, reliable contemporary channels and many others.

The transition into the Fifth Dimension includes preparing the physical body to tolerate the higher frequencies. That is why it is essential to activate the lightbody and construct an ascension vehicle. Too often, people participating in the ascension process lose sight of the fact that **this very much requires a physical change.**

Over the past years there have been other lightbody activation systems and other 12-strand DNA activation methods. The Pleiadians have revealed the way to accomplish changes in a uniquely different and simplified way.

It is no longer required to work with complicated meditations and spiritual practices over years that are difficult for most people to complete. These systems are not wrong. The Beings explained that this is simply the first time that the conditions are right to activate the body from only an energetic level. This energetic 12-strand DNA Activation is an ascension DNA activation and different from other methods.

One of the most remarkable sections of the book is the material in Chapter 9 when the Pleiadian guides define each additional DNA strand (three through twelve) and the etheric changes which take place upon activation. For example, the third DNA strand Activation decommissions the death programming in the body. There is no longer a need to physically die to be reborn. The Shift into the next life is seamless as we change dimensions.

The meanings of all the ten additional DNA strands end with the twelfth. That is the one that activates the personal ascension vehicle.

We should gratefully acknowledge the Pleiadian Beings for this astounding roadmap to ascension. Their skill at placing complex technology within a context of such power, clarity and simplicity bespeaks a consciousness evolved well beyond our own.

The instructions in this book teach you how to do these important activations on your own. They are simple and straightforward. You need not understand the finer points of any metaphysical system or ascension in particular. You need not be psychic. You really need not even be sure that any of this is true or that it works. It is easy to check it out for yourself.

Be sure to understand that the Shift in 2012 is a move into a very different reality from our present Third Dimension life. There will be peace. There will be an enhancement of psychic abilities. Most communication will likely be telepathic. Other profound changes will be commonplace. It is outside the subject of this book to give a lengthy description of the Fifth Dimension. It is mentioned in passing to underscore what is at stake. It holds out the real opportunity to leave behind the world of duality, of light and dark. It has taken millions of years for Earth and all of humanity to step into this brave new world where we can join the galactic community free of the dark things that have made life here a very tough struggle.

Book Three in this series is *Countdown to Ascension* by Diana Stone, Duane's sister and co-author of their first book (expected publication date late 2006). Diana serves an international clientele as a shaman healer and professional astrologer. When this brother-sister team first learned the Fifth Dimension Lightbody Activation method, the big question was: What happens after lightbody? Will everybody be instantly healed of everything? Maybe absolutely nothing will happen. Will some people walk on water? Diana and her husband, Don, field tested the activation for three years before the book was first published to answer this very question.

The answer is that something definitely happens. Logically it is not the same experience for everyone. The most compelling awareness, however, is that it is necessary to focus on one's inner work more rather than less. All of the activations for that matter bring out the issues that need to be dealt with in both one's inner and outer life.

It is obvious that Duane and Diana are bringing together both sides of a very complex process. Based on Duane's relationship with the Pleiadians, he brings through the technology aspect of ascension, the actual techniques. Now it is apparent that personal transition does not "just happen." Diana draws on long experience to describe in *Countdown to Ascension* how to map out your personal journey to the dimensional Shift in 2012.

Many guidelines for healing within the context of the crystal triangle are successfully used by professional healers and beginners alike. These include dealing with toxic relationships, invading dark entities, past life influences, body memories of past wounds, ancestral patterns and the like. ***When Duane does the Four Activations, an invaluable aspect of his work is the clearing of blocks along with them.*** Some of his cases are included in this book.

Where Are We Now?

A significant shift in the Mayan calendar marked the beginning of one of the most important cycles in history. This came to be known as the Breakthrough Ceremony and was observed May 27-28, 2006. Duane journeyed with his shamanic troupe with whom he has worked for over 25 years and was surprised to download the early pieces of what appears to be the beginnings of yet another book in this series.

At this point the new information is clearly associated with the heart and heart chakra. The alignments extend beyond Planet Earth to line up with our Sun, our Galactic Center in the Milky Way galaxy and even beyond to the Great Central Sun of the Creator. At this very early stage of working out this new system, there are already four pieces to the Heart Activation. Duane has experimented using this new protocol with several clients and they reported extremely powerful reactions. It is difficult to jump to conclusions at this point; however, there are clues that a powerful new healing system may be in progress. Watch the Web sites (www.dianastone.com and www.duanehenkle.com) or subscribe to Duane or Diana's free newsletters to keep abreast of exciting new developments.

July 10, 2006

Preface

Preface

There are a few questions that have been consistently raised by lecture audiences and readers. For the sake of clarity, these confusing issues are best addressed before you read the book.

The ascension process should not be confused with the Rapture described in the Christian Bible. They are not the same at all.

The DNA Activations described in this book refer to changes in the etheric body not the physical body. There may well be measurable changes in the physical DNA at some point, however, no reliable sources have been found that could substantiate that before this book was published.

Other questions concern the Fourth Dimension. What happened to it? The Pleiadians and most other writers agree that the Shift is indeed into the Fifth Dimension. It is at the Fifth Dimension level that the wheel of rebirth no longer turns; yet reincarnation still occurs from the Fourth Dimension. A likely explanation is that everyone is functioning in a consciousness at various levels. Some people are in the lower levels of the Fourth Dimension and yet others are at the higher frequencies of the Fourth Dimension and may even occasionally cross over.

Some advanced individuals access the Fifth Dimension frequently.

At the time of the Shift, everybody goes somewhere that matches their rung on the evolutionary ladder and that may not mean a shift to the Fifth Dimension.

It is important to stay aware that the ascension process and the complex workings of great evolutionary forces are never going to be completely understood by our little brains in the Third Dimension. The Pleiadian Beings were never given to long technical explanations. Their genius absolutely lies in the straight forward methods that have been given to us as simple tools that can be used by almost anybody. We probably cannot fully appreciate the wisdom this reveals.

Chapter One

The Story of the Fifth Dimension Lightbody Activation

The Story of the Fifth Dimension Lightbody Activation

A mystery number is one that appears repeatedly in the process of solving a complex mathematics problem, popping up time and again without apparent rhyme or reason. An observant individual, however, realizes that this recurring number is casting light on the solution to the problem in some mysterious way, and consequently, peeks beneath the surface in an effort to discover what particular truth is trying to emerge.

Mystery Crystals

In much the same way, crystals began popping up in my life. It took me years to understand that these mystery crystals were revealing a great truth about my life. Now, of course, I understand. My mission in this life is to bring in the Four Activations that prepare us for ascension in 2012, learn how to do them myself, and then share with others how it's done. Crystals are significant because a crystal layout placed around the body powers each of the Four Activations.

My first crystal encounter occurred in 1985, when I was in the early stages of a spiritual awakening. Mine was a case of arrested development since I was into my forties when the bell tolled. Always a reader, I discovered metaphysical literature and began devouring these books with a ravenous appetite. Many of these books probed the world of spirit guides and their authors wrote movingly of personal experiences with Helpers beyond the veil.

I was overwhelmed by the possibility that my own personal spirit guides may just be waiting to assist *me* in achieving *my* mission. I began a series of late night meditations, an hour or so in duration, in order to connect. After several months of trying, one night I succeeded—yes, with tears streaming down my face, I succeeded.

My guide was sitting on a ledge overlooking a little stream, so deep in the forest only slivers of sunlight peeked through the trees. I could smell the damp vegetation underfoot. And there sat my guide, a Trickster if I ever saw one, just watching me with a twinkle in his eye. He was dressed in clothes from another time—Atlantis perhaps. A turban was wrapped around his head. And right where the turban covered his Third Eye was a small green crystal. It was in a natural, unpolished state, yet it caught my eye. We didn't talk much that night, just made introductions, but the image of that crystal on his Third Eye seemed oddly significant and remained etched into my memory.

My second crystal encounter occurred about a year later. My sister, Diana, and I had flown to Texas to visit Dad who wintered in the Rio Grande Valley. At the end of that trip, she produced a cloth in which were wrapped two green unpolished crystals. These were smallish crystals that fit in the palm of your hand.

Diana told a rather bizarre tale as to how these crystals came into her possession. At an astrology conference (Diana is a professional astrologer, among other things), an acquaintance, also attending the conference, spotted Diana and gave her the crystals, saying she didn't want to do it, but her spirit guide gave explicit orders that she should. She handed over the two crystals, explaining that they had come from the base of a pyramid in Egypt and were among her prized possessions.

The Shaman Path Calls

The woman's guide had a message, namely that Diana would keep one crystal for herself and give the other to a person with whom she would work. Further, that person should hold the crystal up to sunlight, and if they could turn it into light, then the door was open for that person to follow the shaman path. If the person chose to follow the shaman path, then they should prick their finger with a pin, put three drops of blood on the crystal and say, "I now follow the shaman path." The guide warned that once taken, the vow could not be reversed. That person was headed down the shaman path—period.

Diana presented one of the crystals to me. Six months later I held it up to bright sunlight, went into an altered state, and turned it into bright, yellow-orange light. I did the drops of blood and the vow. Yes, that green crystal was identical to the one on my guide's turban!

My next crystal encounter took the form of a vision that lasted several hours while I sat transfixed on my living room floor. My spirit guide took me into a mountain cave for training and when I came out several years later, I was carrying a set of crystals he had bestowed upon me at graduation. These crystals had the power to transform consciousness. I trained others in their use in much the same way that my guide had trained me, and upon completion, bestowed a set of crystals upon each graduate.

I was entrenched in the corporate world at the time, in the middle of a divorce after a marriage of almost thirty years, and really didn't understand this vision. I had spiritually awakened—yes—but going into a cave with my spirit guide and emerging years later with crystals was beyond my capacity to grasp.

It never occurred to me that my shaman path might take a detour though the Valley of the Shadow. I envisioned a smooth, ascending road with a friendly sign reading, "Pass Go, Collect $200." Had I known what lay ahead, I may not have pricked my finger and taken the shaman vow. I spent several years roaming around in the Valley of the Shadow, battling serious physical illness brought on by inhaling too many toxic insecticides working in the crop fields of Iowa as a youth. I eventually was healed and could remember my name again; my brain having recovered after a long, arduous stint of rehabilitation therapy.

Hawaii Calls

So I survived the Valley of the Shadow and emerged on the other side—now what?

What is my purpose? Why am I here? I asked Spirit for help because the fog was so thick I couldn't see six feet down the road. Spirit answered.

I was impinged to pull up stakes and move to Hawaii. That threw me into a state of total confusion. Not long after, a woman from my past walked out of the fog. We had once been close and then I had moved away. The attraction was still there and we began seeing each other again. A few months later I totally lost my reason, called her up on the phone and asked her to 1) move to Hawaii and 2) live with me. She said yes to both questions. (Spirit whispered into her ear also.)

Then my brain kicked in. What if this turned out to be the stupidest move of my entire life? A lot of things could go wrong here! I got out my sacred *I Ching* book and coins. I wrote out my request on a sheet of paper: "Please comment on my moving to Hawaii." I flipped the coins and formed the hexagram: *No. 1—Creative Power* changing into *No. 14—Sovereignty.*

The first paragraph of the *Creative Power* hexagram read: *"Creative Power* is nothing less than the detonating device in the evolutionary bomb. The time is exceptional in terms of inspiration, energy and will. It could be compared to the generative power of the creation when the sperm enters and quickens the egg. The force of this time is the primal directive that propels us into our destinies regardless of what our reasoning or recalcitrant minds may think."

The first paragraph of the *Sovereignty* hexagram read: "Because of a stroke of good fortune you will meet with supreme success. At few times do you possess more. Seldom are you able to receive as much. Your position has become one of authority within the situation of your inquiry, yet you continue in an attitude of unassuming modesty. With such an attitude you pose no threat to those and they, therefore, loyally align themselves to your authority. Thus you are granted *SOVERIEGNTY.* This power should be controlled with moderation and modesty, leading you into a state of great progress and potential."

The power of the reading stunned me! I thought *romance* was carrying my soon-to-be partner and me to Hawaii, but now I realized that something larger was happening. *What is my purpose? Why am I here?* My questions had been heard after all, and now the answers were beginning to unfold in my life. I was giddy with anticipation as I sold off my household furniture in preparation for the move to the Big Island where we had decided to live. Unbeknownst to me, my next crystal encounter was waiting for me there.

The Pleiadian Walk-in

The Big Island of Hawaii was like Paradise—with a lot of black lava rock thrown in. This one island comprised half the landmass of the entire Hawaiian chain, yet the population numbered only 130,000. By contrast, the island of Oahu, which included the city of Honolulu, had a population well over one million. Life was simple, easy and uncomplicated for the first few months. And then the message came through that I was going to be the recipient of a Pleiadian walk-in soul. Previously, my spirit guide had trained me to assist him in the process of bringing in a number of walk-in souls, plus I had read several books on the subject including Ruth Montgomery's popular *Aliens Among Us*. I had no fear of this and welcomed the energetic upgrade. A few nights later, I stretched out on the bed and closed my eyes as my partner worked in my energy field. She followed the precise instructions that I had carefully channeled and translated to 3"x5" index cards. The deed was done.

The Search for the Land Triangle

Almost immediately, my intuitive powers took an exponential leap. I could now visualize a person, scan their energy field, diagnose blocks and clear them. Visions of triangles—not sugarplums—danced in my head as I strained to understand their meaning. Over a period of several months, a knowingness began to surface from deep within my core: *A triangle of land existed somewhere on the island that enclosed a powerful vortex of energy.*

Finding this area became my obsession in life. I finally located it after months of searching—a narrow triangle of land about thirty miles long and four miles wide at the base. There were placeholders anchoring the energy at the three points of the triangle.

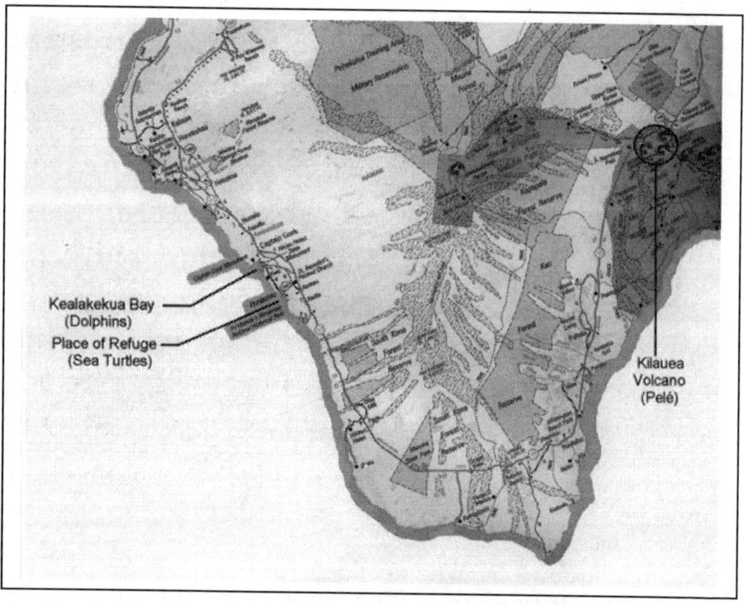

Hawaii, the Big Island, Showing the Land Triangle and Energy Points of Pele, Dolphin and Sea Turtle

The apex of the triangle was Kilauea Volcano, which was home to Pele, the powerful Hawaiian Goddess of Fire. Thirty miles away at the ocean shoreline was the sacred place of Pu'u Honua O Honaunau, now a national historic park, where the sea turtles in the bay anchored the energy at the left base of the triangle. The right base of the triangle was located four miles up the shoreline at Kealakekua Bay, a federal underwater sanctuary, where large numbers of dolphins anchored the energy there.

Shortly thereafter, I walked into a metaphysical store full of beautiful, expensive crystals—*and into the midst of my next crystal encounter!* Understanding exploded in my mind like a burst of 4th of July fireworks. I visualized a crystal triangle in my living room that duplicated in miniature the powerful energies of the actual land triangle! I bought a big amethyst geode for the Pele crystal, a three-pound fluorite crystal flawlessly sculpted into the likeness of Sea Turtle and a beautiful three-pound rose quartz crystal sculpted into the likeness of Dolphin.

Pleiadian Physics 101

Shortly following this mind-altering leap in consciousness, a small group of Pleiadian entities contacted me psychically with a message: “Set up the Crystal Triangle in your living room and we will teach you how to use it in order to activate the lightbody in preparation for the coming shift to the Fifth Dimension in 2012. We will teach you according to our higher laws of physics. Don’t be too impressed—this is really just Pleiadian Physics 101.”

An intensive training period ensued that lasted many months. My partner and I positioned ourselves inside the Crystal Triangle. I was shown a mental picture of a specific movement to make in the energy field. I mimicked this movement in my partner’s energy field. We took turns practicing on each other. Then, on to the next mental picture. We knew we were on to something, as the energies of Lightbody Activation nearly blasted us into the next dimension!

We bought a three-story, 5000-square-foot house on a mountain slope overlooking the ocean and, after a year’s work, turned it into a small healing center and bed-and-breakfast with three ocean-view sleeping rooms. It was mid-1999 and almost three years had passed since moving to Hawaii. *What is my purpose? Why am I here?* Those questions had now been answered and it was time for me to move on.

My partner and I agreed to an amicable parting. She stayed to manage the place as sole owner and I moved back to Santa Fe, New Mexico. A week before leaving, I went into an altered state of consciousness and was advised that the walk-in soul had departed — its mission with me completed. Years later, I came across information that reinforced the wisdom of my Pleiadian friends in guiding me to the power triangle on the Big Island of Hawaii.

Richard Hoagland was a NASA scientist and researcher involved in the satellite mission to Mars. He wrote a book that has become fairly well known in scientific and metaphysical circles, *The Monuments on Mars.* He has the satellite photos that appear to prove that, yes indeed; somebody built pyramids on Mars similar to those on Earth. Of course, this remains controversial. Read his book and see what you think of the implications if this is true!

Hoagland presents a strong case that hidden geometries of energy surrounding the planets in our solar system create vortices of energy at points where the geometric lines intersect. That's why the planets, including Earth, exhibit powerful energy vortices at 19.5 degrees north latitude and 19.5 degrees south latitude. Nineteen and one-half degrees north latitude passes right through the Big

Island of Hawaii and Hoagland verifies that powerful energies are swirling around on the Big Island. I believe the exact vortex point is Kilauea Volcano, home to Pele, the Hawaiian Goddess of Fire. Keep in mind—a Pele crystal resides at the apex of the Crystal Triangle.

Beginning Work with Crystal Triangle

I was finding my niche in life. Back in Santa Fe, New Mexico, I opened a full-time practice doing energy healing and Lightbody Activation. The Crystal Triangle Lightbody Activation Method calls for two people, the one giving the activation and the one receiving the activation. A triangle of crystals is placed around the Receiver. The Giver performs nine prescribed movements in the energy field of the Receiver. Along the way, the Receiver recites several key affirmations. Complete instructions with illustrations are in my first book, *The Lightbody Activation Manual*. For your convenience, they are also included in this book in their entirety.

Chapter Two

The Story of the Sixth Dimension Activation

The Story of the Sixth Dimension Activation

Time passed since my Hawaii sojourn—it was now 2003. My work doing energy clearing and Lightbody Activation was on the upswing. In addition to personal clients from the local Santa Fe area, I was reaching a growing number of telephone clients that stretched across the United States. Telephone sessions were similar to those in person. The work from a remote location quickly proved to be as equally effective as in-person work!

Over a period of eighteen months, I wrote a book titled *The Light-body Activation Manual,* which was now making inroads in metaphysical bookstores across the country. The book covered energy clearing and the Crystal Triangle Lightbody Activation Method. My sister, Diana Stone, a successful writer, astrologer and shaman for many years, was the co-author.

The extraterrestrial advisors didn't seem to have any more clever activation techniques up their sleeves. They were content, evidently, stepping into the background and acting as advisors during my interactions with clients. That was okay with me because I was in the flow: good job, good clients, good guides. Who could ask for more?

I crossed paths with John, an interesting man who was very adept in his work as an acupuncturist and energy healer. We became friends and began doing trades on a weekly basis. I had a sufficient number of physical aches and pains to keep him occupied well into the future. My younger associate had almost no physical complaints to speak of, so I concentrated on activating his lightbody—again and again and again. I had now activated his lightbody for the eighth week in a row and was scratching my head about what to do next.

Meeting the Metatron Man

That's when the Pleiadians stepped forward and began relaying mental images in much the same way as they had done in Hawaii. I focused intently on the connection so as not to miss whatever it was they had decided to show me. To an observer, John was stretched out on the energy table and I was guiding him through a visualization. Actually, the Pleiadians were guiding us both through a visualization that I was describing aloud. I came to realize that doing this aloud locked the steps of the process into my memory so I could write about them later.

I was in the Fifth Dimension. The voice said that this was the realm of Archangel Michael. I was walking around in my lightbody, which had the appearance of a billion particles of light arranged in the form of a human body. The voice told me to approach the Sixth Dimension veil and I did so. The veil appeared as a matrix of light. I couldn't see or pass through it, but I knew the Sixth Dimension was on the other side.

The voice informed me that in going to the Sixth Dimension, I left the realm of Archangel Michael and entered the realm of Archangel Metatron, a very high being who sits alongside the Great Creator. Archangel Metatron exists at a vibration level well above the Sixth Dimension, but he can step down an aspect of himself into the Sixth Dimension frequency. This aspect is called the Metatron Man and he was waiting for me on the other side of the veil. I was to stand before the veil, peer through until I saw him on the other side, then pass through and merge my lightbody with the Metatron Man.

Now You See Him, Now You Don't

I followed instructions, passed through the veil and tried merging myself with the Metatron Man. The energy was so intense I could hold it for only a few seconds and then found myself bouncing back into the Fifth Dimension. The voice then led me back to Earth. I maneuvered my body so that I landed with my heart chakra right on the Four Corners, which is the geographical intersection point of the borders of four states—Arizona, Colorado, Utah and New Mexico. I was informed that the intersecting lines of the Four Corners were the physical manifestation of a solar cross formed by the intersecting lines of the energy grid above the surface of Earth. Further, the intersection point of the solar cross created a vortex of Sixth Dimension energy and therefore, by landing on Earth with my heart chakra directly on the Four Corners, I was actually receiving a Sixth Dimension Activation.

Over the next month, John and I repeated this process until we were able to merge with the Metatron Man and hold the energy. In this dimension, my lightbody still took the form of a human body but the particles of light were brighter and more highly energized—literally dancing around. After each session, I returned to Earth by way of the Four Corners, landing on the exact intersection point and receiving another shot of Sixth Dimension energy in my heart chakra.

Time to Crunch the Numbers

I was puzzled. For several years I had been doing energy clearing and Lightbody Activation without a word from the Beings about anything else. In my mind, this was it until 2012 and the Big Shift. I had even written a book—and that seemed to tie a ribbon around the whole subject.

Now the Pleiadians were talking numbers. I was not simply doing Lightbody Activations. I was doing Fifth Dimension Lightbody Activations. It was obvious that they were deliberately focusing on the dimension number. Now they were walking me through the veil into the Sixth Dimension. "*Be aware of the number, Duane,*" they said, while merging me with an entity called the Metatron Man. They always returned me to Earth by way of the Four Corners where my heart chakra received another shot of Sixth Dimension energy. Why was I doing this? Was I supposed to be doing this with other people?

I decided to find out. I had a regular client who had been seeing me once a month for the past six months. He made another appointment. We did our usual energy clearing and Lightbody Activation—uh, Fifth Dimension Lightbody Activation, that is. And then I led him through the questionable Sixth Dimension visualization. Somewhere over the

Four Corners area of the United States, the entire session ground to a halt. My client left that session in a state of confusion and skepticism, to say the least, and didn't come back any time soon. I informed the Beings that if they expected me to do the Sixth Dimension whatcha-ma-callit with clients, they had better get their heads together and come up with something simpler.

Discovering the Cross of Light

A week later, another client, whom I considered a prime candidate for the journey into the Sixth Dimension, scheduled an appointment. She eagerly agreed to give it a try. During the session, I did the usual energy clearing and then the Fifth Dimension Lightbody Activation. I sat with my head bowed, just waiting and trying to cancel all thoughts of the Metatron Man and the Four Corners area of the United States. Suddenly, a whole new set of mental images came clearly to mind. Several minutes passed while I sorted it all out.

My client was lying on her back on my energy table surrounded by the triangle of three crystals used for the Fifth Dimension Lightbody Activation. I was directed to place the Sixth Dimension crystal layout around her body: 1) a programmed feminine energy crystal went behind her head at the North Pole, 2) a programmed masculine energy crystal went below her feet at the South Pole, 3) a programmed feminine energy crystal went to her left side in line with her chest at the East Pole and 4) a programmed masculine energy crystal went to her right side in line with her chest at the West Pole.

In this layout, the energy runs from north to south and from east to west. Therefore, the predominant poles are North and East, both of which are feminine in nature. That's different from the present dimension, which has a masculine orientation. "Must be the Goddess rebalancing things," I mused.

Then I was directed to say, "With a laser beam of light down the center line of your body, connect the North Pole crystal beyond your head with the South Pole crystal beyond your feet. See the laser beam on the surface of your body.

"With a laser beam of light across your chest, connect the East Pole crystal on your left with the West Pole crystal on your right. See the laser beam on the surface of your body.

"What you have formed on your body is a *cross of light.* The intersection of the cross creates a vortex of Sixth Dimension energy. The intersection point is now located right on your heart. Your heart chakra is now activating with Sixth Dimension energy. This is the energy of Archangel Metatron."

Then, in tandem, I lowered the crystals at her right and left, in line with the sexual chakra at the base of the spine. Then I said, "I've lowered the cross to intersect with the first chakra. See the laser beam cross there, as your first chakra activates with Sixth Dimension energy."

Then, I moved the side crystals upward one chakra at a time, moving the cross upward and activating each chakra as I went. I skipped over the heart on the way up because that chakra was activated first.

After activating all seven body chakras, I said, "I am raising the cross beyond the crown chakra and activating the eighth chakra."

And finally, "I'm raising the cross one last time, to a position beyond the eighth chakra. As the cross rests in this highest position, Metatron chakras nine, ten and eleven open simultaneously."

My client was buzzing with Sixth Dimension energy at the conclusion of the session. I thanked my Pleiadian guides for their new, streamlined Sixth Dimension version.

The Power of the Sixth Dimension Activation

I soon discovered that this newfound energy from the Sixth Dimension had a variety of uses. I received a phone call from an individual who said that his friend recommended me. The caller had a delicate problem. His job required him to step on the toes of certain people in high places. The people in high places didn't like that and "put a curse on him."

This may have been the reason why he had awakened that morning to the sight of a devil-like entity in his bedroom. After several minutes of world class fright, the caller had the presence of mind to grab the Bible and recite the Twenty-Third Psalm until the nasty creature vacated the premises. The caller feared another encounter and, on the advice of his friend who had been a client of mine, gave me a call. I told the caller I would do my best to clear his house.

I went into a meditative state in order to survey the scene and determine what to do. A series of images came into my mind that bore the stamp of my friends in the Pleiades. I thought it was the bsetter part of wisdom to follow their direction without reservation. I called the man back and did the Sixth Dimension Activation on all his chakras using the laser beam cross (once again, this was all from a remote location). Then I instructed him to get four crystals and place them in the north, south, east and west corners of the room, thus establishing the four poles. Then, using a laser beam of light and following my instructions, he connected the North Pole to the South Pole and the East Pole to the West Pole, forming a laser beam cross in his living room.

He determined the intersection point of the cross and marked it on the floor. Then he sat right on that spot and soaked up the protective energy of the Sixth Dimension. I called several days later to check on him. The bad entity was gone but my client was taking no chances. He was on the "hotspot" with his pillow and his blanket and wasn't about to leave!

Chapter Three

The Story of the Seventh Dimension Activation

The Story of the Seventh Dimension Activation

My acupuncturist buddy and I continued to trade sessions back and forth. He was once again stretched out on my energy table. I did some energy clearing, followed by the Fifth Dimension Lightbody Activation and then the new Sixth Dimension Activation. To an observer, I was leading my partner through a visualization, but in actuality the Pleiadian helpers were once again guiding us both through the visualization that I was describing aloud.

How Do You Get Through This Thing?

I was walking around in the Sixth Dimension. The key to this dimension was learning to merge with and hold the energy of the Metatron Man. After several months of training, I finally got the hang of it. The Pleiadians asked, “What would you think about taking a trip into the *Seventh* Dimension?” Here they were talking numbers again. I didn't bother to answer their obvious rhetorical question.

Ready or not, I was headed for the Seventh Dimension. More instructions: “Find the Seventh

Dimension veil." I scouted around until I found it at the very edge of the Sixth Dimension—a grid of light so tightly woven that steam could not have passed through it. The thing looked totally impenetrable to me. I informed my advisors that it would be easier for a camel to pass through the eye of a needle than it would be for me to pass through this veil.

More from my guides, "The Seventh Dimension exists at a very high frequency, Duane. No one can connect with this dimension in the same way as the lower dimensions are accessed. As you can see, the grid of light is much too compact for even a lightbody to pass through. *Only your consciousness can pass through.* So, relax the 'glue' that holds the particles of your lightbody together and, at the same time, project your consciousness through the veil."

I tried that several times and nothing happened. I tried again—and kazaam—I shot through the veil into the Seventh Dimension! I found myself looking back through the veil into the Sixth Dimension, where a pile of light particles lay that had been my lightbody moments before.

The Dimension of the Quantum Energy Body

My guides then advised, "Even the atoms of your body cannot pass through the veil of the Seventh Dimension, for this is the dimension of quantum or sub-atomic light, of pure photon particles radiating from the Great Central Sun. You have a vehicle in this dimension but not of human shape, as you know it. You are a concentration of free form quantum energy. *You are in the Christ Realm.*"

When it was time to leave, I reversed course back into the Sixth Dimension, then into the Fifth Dimension, then back to Earth and the inevitable landing on the Four Corners intersection point of Arizona, Colorado, Utah, and New Mexico, then back to my healing room. I asked my friend what he thought of the Seventh Dimension and he answered, "Ethereal, very ethereal." I added, "Wow, that place is quiet." Every week over the next month, we practiced going all the way into the Seventh Dimension. This quantum light energy was very expansive, to say the least, and we always came back feeling refreshed, reenergized and somewhat disoriented.

New Sixth Dimension Activation Method

At this point, there was a streamlined version of the Fifth Dimension Activation by using three crystals placed around the body in the shape of a triangle. Also, there was a streamlined version of the Sixth Dimension Activation by placing four crystals around the body at the North, South, East and West Poles.

So far so good, but what I did not have was a streamlined version of the Seventh Dimension Activation. Not to worry. At the next session, my guides were apparently ready to remedy that situation. "Let us show you how to do this activation using crystals. That way, your clients won't have to go through this business of figuring out how to pass through the veil into the Seventh Dimension."

The Sixth Dimension crystal layout was in place around the table. The guides reminded me, "Now there is a feminine crystal beyond the head at the North Pole, a masculine crystal beyond the feet at the South Pole, a feminine crystal at the left side at the East Pole and a masculine crystal at the right side at the West Pole. Using a laser beam of light to connect the North Pole to the South Pole and the East Pole to the West Pole, a laser beam cross was formed on the body of your friend that activated the energy of the Sixth Dimension."

The New Seventh Dimension Activation Method

The guides continued, *"Now adjust the crystals into the Seventh Dimension crystal layout.* Move the feminine crystal at the East Pole on the left down below the feet to the South Pole along side the masculine crystal. Next, move the masculine crystal at the West Pole on the right up beyond the head to the North Pole along side the feminine crystal. In the Seventh Dimension, there are no East and West Poles—they have been absorbed into oneness by the North and South Poles. Looking at the North and South Poles, we see a feminine crystal and a masculine crystal side by side. These now merge into oneness as there is no feminine-masculine polarity in the Seventh Dimension — there is only unity."

The guides continued, "With a laser beam of light down the center line of the body, connect the unified North Pole with the unified South Pole. As you do this, the North and South Poles open simultaneously and the quantum energy of the Seventh Dimension flows in, surrounding the body in a cloud of pure photon light one hundred feet in diameter.

This flow through the North Pole opens the Alpha chakra above the head. The flow through the South Pole opens the Omega chakra below the feet. These are chakras twelve and thirteen, which must be open in order to ascend into the next dimension."

My friend who was receiving the activation missed all the fireworks. He had conked out during the whole thing. In subsequent sessions, I used this streamlined version to do the Seventh Dimension Activation and he felt plenty. I was quickly very proficient in doing the Fifth Dimension, Sixth Dimension and Seventh Dimension Activations. I thanked the guides for their brilliance in opening the door to the upper dimensions by using simple crystal layouts that almost anyone could duplicate.

The Power of the Seventh Dimension Activation

I soon discovered that the Seventh Dimension Activation had the power to clear a broad range of negative energies. A woman called who I knew to be an adept spiritual healer. She had a large following of clients in the United States and other countries as well. She traveled widely, exercising her spiritual gifts with ten to fifteen clients per day.

She crossed paths with a guru-type man who at first appeared to be a shining light but over time proved to be highly manipulative and negative. She had no choice but to cut off all communication with him, including not taking his phone calls. Now she believed he had placed some sort of hex on her. In recent months her life had taken a sudden turn for the worse. She didn't feel right physically, plus her client business was drying up fast. I scheduled a telephone session with her the next day.

As usual, the consultation via phone was virtually the same as an in-person session. The client reclined on a bed rather than an energy table. I visualized the crystal layouts around her body. We talked back and forth while I facilitated the Fifth Dimension Lightbody Activation.

I kept my inner eye open for some sort of dark connection from the guru guy but, surprisingly, found nothing. Then I placed the four crystals around the woman's body and did the Sixth Dimension Activation using the laser beam cross on all the chakras. Again, I could see no connection of any kind to negative influences. I was puzzled.

Clearing Negative Energies Remotely

Then inspiration struck! I had accessed the Seventh Dimension Activation not long before but had never done it by telephone. Now was the time. I sensed my Pleiadian guides nearby offering help if needed. I adjusted the four crystals into the Seventh Dimension layout. That's when I spotted it—a little black dot bouncing around in her energy field.

What the hell is that thing? My Pleiadian guides answered, "That's a 'virus' in her energy field, placed there by a very adept black magician. A virus in a computer can attack the system and ultimately close it down. A virus in your energy field can attack the meridian system of your body and ultimately close it down. The virus is the most powerful form of negative energy that you'll find. The Seventh Dimension Activation will clear it out."

The guides were right. At the end of the activation, the woman's energy field was clear, showing no sign of the black dot virus. In the weeks that followed, the woman's energy—and her client base—bounced back to normal. The woman then confided that a handful of others had come in contact with the guru guy and bad things were happening in their lives. It turned out that each one had the virus and each one had to be cleared using the Seventh Dimension Activation.

Houses Have Problems Too

Here's another example of the power of the Seventh Dimension Activation to clear negative energy. A woman called who was distraught over how life was going for her and her husband in recent years. Her husband was previously a highly paid CEO. They lived in an expensive luxury home. A contractor they hired to do an extensive remodel on the house had botched it. They fired him. The contractor sued for $100,000 and won in court. That was one thing.

Another thing was that bad luck seemed to follow the husband around in his car. He'd racked up three accidents in three years. To top it all off, he also had lost his high paying job and hadn't found another one in over a year. They were financially in trouble. Her woman's intuition sensed that something was energetically "off" in their lives.

The husband, a conventional guy who wasn't a big believer in invisible energies, was open to calling me because nothing else seemed to work. In desperate times, unconventional methods are sometimes more acceptable! I agreed to examine the situation to see what I could do.

I journeyed inward and took a look at the couple and their surroundings. I discovered an energetic attachment *to the house* by beings hostile to Earth and coming from another dimension. The purpose of the attachment was to energetically take over the residents who lived in the house and eventually use them for their own purposes. That's not a nice scenario to live with—and this couple was experiencing the negative effects every day of their lives.

First I cleared the wife and husband by doing the Fifth, Sixth and Seventh Dimension Activations with each of them. Then I instructed the couple to set up the Seventh Dimension Crystal Layout at the North and South Poles of their property and then connect the two poles with a laser beam of light in order to activate the power of the Seventh Dimension.

This cleared the entire property — including the unwanted energetic attachment to the house — and protected against any future energetic invasions as well.

Negative energy simply cannot penetrate the high frequency of the Seventh Dimension. These "crazy proceedings" pushed the belief system of the husband to the absolute limit, but he hung in there with his wife. That was over a year ago. Today their house remains clear. Trouble doesn't follow them around anymore. The husband landed another very high paying CEO-type job and life prospered for them after that.

Eight Dimension Model of the Universe

The Pleiadians had now revealed activations all the way to the Seventh Dimension. Just how close to the top was that? How many dimensions are there? How high is *up?* It became clear that my guides were not going to indulge me with a long, theoretical discussion of the dimensions. Our work together was obviously more practical in nature, centering on the steps involved in doing the Fifth, Sixth and Seventh Dimension Activations. But I was told the following: Earth is presently in the Third Dimension, passing through the Fourth Dimension and preparing to shift into the Fifth Dimension in 2012. There are eight dimensions in total—and many, many subdivisions within each. The Eighth Dimension cannot be breached at this time.

So I looked elsewhere to satisfy my curiosity about the dimensions, which was most likely the intention of my guides in the first place.

Approximately one year later, I happened upon a Web site on the Internet that was everything I'd ever dreamed of in regard to explaining the nature of reality, the workings of the dimensions and the upcoming Ascension or dimensional shift.

The Web site—www.ascension2000.com—is the work of a remarkable individual named David Wilcock. In addition to being a high-level channel in his own right, he has spent years researching some of the best channeled material to ever hit this planet, namely the Edgar Cayce readings, the Seth Material by Jane Roberts and The Law of One material by Ra, a "group memory complex" (note: similar to group mind) from the Sixth Dimension.

Spirit and Science Merge

Furthermore, Mr. Wilcock possesses the necessary knowledge, background and training to research the scientific studies and experiments that probe these same subjects. The result is a paradigm-changing view of the nature of reality, the workings of the dimensions and the upcoming dimensional shift *supported by both the spiritual and the scientific communities*. This remarkable synthesis is included on his Web site in various articles and three on-line books. I've printed them for my own study – over 800 pages to date – and have them housed in four voluminous three-ring binders.

According to Wilcock's information, we live in a universe of eight dimensions. These eight dimensions form the Octave, similar to the sound octave of eight notes in the diatonic musical scale—*do, re, mi, fa, so, la, ti, do*. There are the seven major notes—*do, re, me, fa, so, la, ti.* And then there is *do* again, representng the Alpha and the Omega, the beginning and the end. It is interesting to note that Plato, the ancient Greek philosopher, referred to the dimensions as "frozen music." In addition to sound, the dimensions also display properties of color and geometry in support of an eight-dimension model of the universe. I won't repeat that information here, but if you want to delve deeper, the Web site is there for you.

It also includes a Law of One Study Guide, a professionally prepared summary of the four Law of One books channeled from Ra during the 1980s. Keep in mind, Ra is a group mind complex channeled from the Sixth Dimension—a level millions of years more advanced than our Third Dimension. Even so, when asked about the Eighth Dimension, Ra spoke of this as the highest dimension—the Octave, the Oneness, All There Is—"*a place of mystery and wonder even for us.*"

The Wilcock information confirmed the Pleiadian guides similar views of the dimensions and the workings of the universe. They had revealed activations all the way to the Seventh Dimension. *That was as high as we could go.* When asked about the number of dimensions, they had answered, *"There are eight dimensions in total."* When asked about the Eighth Dimension, they had answered, *"The Eighth Dimension cannot be breached."* They had given all the right answers.

Chapter Four

The Story of the 12-Strand DNA Activation

The Story of the 12-Strand DNA Activation

This present journey began in Hawaii in 1997 when I accessed the Fifth Dimension Lightbody Activation from my Pleiadian guides. Then, early in 2003, more information started rolling in as I accessed the Sixth Dimension Activation and then the Seventh Dimension Activation. It was now the fall of 2003 and I figured this surely was it. Since the Seventh Dimension was the limit as to how high we could go, then what else could there be?

The status quo would probably hold for some time. Then I began hearing about Harmonic Concordance—an ascension event marked by a rare Star of David configuration in the heavens and triggered by a solar eclipse on either November 8 or 9, depending on your location on the globe. Additional significance for me was the fact that my birthday fell on November 9. In metaphysical circles, it was believed that this was a time of a significant shift to a higher frequency for Earth and its peoples. Back in August of 1987, Harmonic Convergence marked Earth entering a probable future of Ascension (or dimensional shift) rather than one of destruction as had occurred in Atlantis and other places at other times in the distant past. And now the other bookend—Harmonic Concordance—was falling neatly into place.

Harmonic Concordance – A Day to Remember

Diana, my sister who is the astrologer in the family, first brought Harmonic Concordance to my attention and was the one who first became aware of the astrological and metaphysical ramifications. She suggested (insisted) I fly to Vancouver, Washington where she lives so that our little spiritual group of four could be together and ready to help anchor the energies.

Our practice over the past twenty years was to get together for such events, and believe me when I say it was not unusual for spiritual fireworks to explode in our midst during such occasions! Diana's spirit guide had been talking about Harmonic Concordance for several months and indicated that information about DNA and group mind would come through at our get-together. One does not take such messages lightly. Plus, I had a daughter, son-in-law and granddaughter approaching her first birthday right across the Columbia River in Portland whom I had not seen recently. I made travel plans immediately.

The day arrived and found the four of us sitting around in the family room. We certainly had our own way of doing things. To an observer, nothing serious was going on, just four friends talking and laughing, drinking wine and an occasional shot of something stronger. But underneath it all, a shamanic ritual was taking place, one very familiar to the participants involved. Late morning turned into afternoon as the hours passed by. Around four o'clock, Diana said, "Something's going on. I feel things starting to move." Minutes passed. I began feeling waves of energy fluttering through my body causing me to shiver.

It should be noted that Diana publishes a monthly e-mail newsletter for her many clients in the United States and beyond. As Harmonic Concordance approached, Diana informed her readers about our group getting together and the information her guide said would come through. She promised her readers a post-Harmonic Concordance edition that would satisfy everyone's curiosity about what actually transpired at her house.

12-Strand DNA Activation Revealed

I continued to feel a fluttering of energy going through my body and began expounding on some DNA information I'd recently come across. For effect, I may have even made several twisting DNA helix movements through the air with my hands. Then I paused. Perhaps I had just delivered my major message for the day. Diana was seated nearby in her big easy chair. She looked at me and said, "If you think that's enough for my next newsletter, Duane, you are sadly mistaken. You'd better come up with a lot more than that."

That got me. Why was *I* the one who had to come up with the DNA stuff for *her* newsletter! Well, great, I'll just make something up. With that, I motioned for David to lie down on the carpet. Then I said, "We're doing a DNA activation here. The eight master cells of the body are located in the thymus gland or high heart. I'm going to go in there and change those eight cells from 2-strand DNA to 12-strand DNA. Over time, these master cells will pass on the change to all the cells in the body. That's how it's done."

Then, making pulling motions extending from his chest, I visualized drawing out 10 additional DNA strands out of each of the eight master cells of his thymus. I was on automatic pilot by this time, as some higher energy had overtaken me. I didn't know what I was doing but I was doing something—with considerable effect.

When I asked David how he was doing he could barely nod his head—the energy had pinned him to the floor. I repeated the process on Diana right in the easy chair where she sat. I remember her groaning and saying, "This is about all I can handle." Diana did the DNA Activation for me. Then I repeated the DNA Activation for Don as he sat in his chair. That just about did me in for the day, but I knew this: Diana had her exclusive DNA story for the next newsletter!

As with the other activations, I was looking for a simplified method using crystals. Unbeknownst to me, Don had videotaped the DNA episode that took place in his family room. That proved to be helpful since my memory of what happened was foggy at best. I had many clarifying conversations with Diana and Don, and with the Pleiadian guides, the same ones who had overtaken me on Harmonic Concordance. Furthermore, I had a steady flow of clients—both in person and by telephone—with whom I could experiment and fine tune the activation method. Over the course of several months, a process evolved similar to those used for the other activations.

The 12-strand DNA Activation could not take place until an individual's consciousness was raised step by step to the Seventh Dimension level. That was no problem—it simply meant that the

DNA Activation must be preceded by the Fifth, Sixth and Seventh Dimension Activations *in that order*. So when a client received the DNA Activation, they actually received all four activations—the preceding three *in sequence* and then the DNA Activation. The Beings insisted the DNA Activation be done just that way.

The Complete DNA Activation

The finalized DNA crystal layout was simple yet powerful. I was guided to buy a set of eight rose quartz crystals, roughly rounded, each one an inch more or less in diameter. I placed the first crystal on the client's upper chest, above the heart and below the throat, right where the thymus is located inside the body.

The client said an affirmation: "I am activating 12-strand DNA in my first master cell." Then, making a pulling motion on each count of 1 through 10, I pulled 10 additional strands of DNA out of the crystal resting on the client's chest. This crystal, in turn, changed the DNA strand count in the first master cell of the thymus gland.

In like manner, one at a time, all eight master cells of the thymus were changed from 2-strand DNA to 12-strand DNA. At the end, all eight crystals were resting on the chest of the client.

Then, I thumped the thymus three times with my fist to set off the activation. When I did this, most clients felt a subtle burst of energy in the thymus that spread outward through the chest. That was it—the 12-strand DNA Activation was off and running.

I know just enough about DNA to do the work I do—and that's about it. I'll leave the complicated technical scientific explanations to the geneticists of the world. However, I have had a deep, deep curiosity about what happens when each of the additional strands of DNA activate in the cells of the body. My clients do too.

I asked the advisors for an explanation. Nothing was forthcoming. I assumed that the subject matter must be too complicated for my third dimensional sensibilities.

However, one day, while leisurely glancing out my glass patio doors at the 10,000 foot. Sangre de Christo Mountains in the distance, I was startled out of my reverie by an unmistakable message from you know who. "We're going to give you some information about DNA strands."

That unceremonious announcement belied the fact that it may well be the first time — at least in recent history — that this information has ever been explained so specifically

The meaning and function of each of the DNA strands 3-12 follows in a special section of this book.

But first, a review of what we know up to this point.

1. *At present, humanity on Earth has 2-strand DNA in the cells of the body. Through the 12-strand DNA Activation, 10 additional strands are activated in the body cells. The 10 additional DNA strands activate one strand at a time.*

2. *First, the third DNA strand activates throughout all the many cells of the body. Then and only then, the fourth DNA strand activates throughout all the many cells of the body. So it progresses through strands 5-6-7-8-9-10-11-12. The additional DNA strands are of a magnetic, multi-dimensional nature and cannot be detected by present scientific equipment. We assume that the changes initially occur in the etheric body.*

3. *It is these additional strands of DNA that trigger the countless number of cellular activities necessary to change our dense physical body into a physical-etheric body. It is these additional strands of DNA that trigger the countless changes necessary to transform our energy field. <u>It is these additional strands of DNA that trigger the change of our total being into an Ascension Vehicle that will carry us to the Fifth Dimension.</u>*

The Pleiadian Guides Explain the Meaning and Function of Each Individual Etheric DNA Strand

The Meaning and Function of the Third Strand DNA Activation.

The death programming in the body is removed.

For every life we live, the circumstances of our death are programmed into cellular memory. In the Fifth Dimension, there is no reincarnation cycle of death and rebirth. We are in our lightbody, and the lifespan is many thousands of years. It prepares us for life in the Fifth Dimension where death programming, as we know it, does not exist.

The Meaning and Function of the Fourth Strand DNA Activation.

The Fifth Dimension light filter on the Third Eye is dissolved.

This allows us to begin receiving the Light Language from the Fifth Dimension. The Third Eye has this capability, as it is a receptor-prism. The Light Language carries instructions to body cells about changing the physical body into a physical-etheric body. Additional information flows into our conscious mind. We are living in one dimension and directly receiving information from another. We are now experiencing life multi-dimensionally.

The Meaning and Function of the Fifth Strand DNA Activation.

The Fifth Dimension light filter on the Heart Chakra is dissolved.

This means that the information we access through our Third Eye is expressed through action in a loving, heartfelt way. The 4th and 5th strands go hand in hand.

The Meaning and Function of the Sixth Strand DNA Activation.

The Sixth Dimension light filter on the Third Eye is dissolved.

This allows us to begin receiving the Light Language from the Sixth Dimension. This Light Language continues to feed information to the body cells regarding transformation into a physical-etheric being. Sixth Dimension information begins to flow into our conscious mind. We are living in one dimension and directly receiving information from two more. We plunge deeper into experiencing life multi-dimensionally.

The Meaning and Function of the Seventh Strand DNA Activation.

The Sixth Dimension light filter on the Heart Chakra is dissolved.

Again, that ensures that the information we access through our Third Eye is expressed through action in a loving, heartfelt way. The 6th and 7th strands go hand in hand.

The Meaning and Function of the Eighth Strand DNA Activation.

The Seventh Dimension light filter on the Third Eye Chakra is dissolved.

This allows us to begin receiving the Light Language from the Seventh Dimension. The Light Language feeds more information into the body cells regarding transformation into a physical-etheric being. Seventh Dimension information begins to flow into our conscious minds. Now we are receiving instructions directly from the quantum Christ Realm.

Christ came to Earth to teach us how to do exactly this—change our bodies into light and ascend into a higher dimension. That original teaching, of course, has been greatly distorted on Earth. We are now living in one dimension and directly receiving information from three more.

We are experiencing life multi-dimensionally as deeply as we can from our vantage point on this side of the veil.

The Meaning and Function of the Ninth Strand DNA Activation.

The Seventh Dimension light filter on the Heart Chakra is dissolved.

This ensures that the information we access through our Third Eye is expressed through actions of *unconditional love.* The 8th and 9th strands go hand in hand.

THE LAST THREE STRANDS POSSESS ASCENSION MAGIC.

The Meaning and Function of the Tenth Strand DNA Activation.

Your ascension vehicle activates.

In the Seventh Dimension Activation, the North and South Poles opened to a flow of quantum Christ energy surrounding the body in a 100-foot diameter cloud. When the 10th strand activates, what's known as the Metatron Matrix forms around the cloud containing it like a vessel so it does not dissipate. *Your Individual Ascension Vehicle is now completely formed.*

The Meaning and Function of the Eleventh Strand DNA Activation.

A Planetary Ascension Vehicle has also formed around Mother Earth.

Now, as the 11th strand activates, lines of light connect your Individual Ascension Vehicle to Mother Earth's, from your North Pole to Earth's North Pole and from your South Pole to Earth's South Pole.

The Meaning and Function of the Twelfth Strand DNA Activation.

As the 12th strand activates, your Individual Ascension Vehicle is charged by a continuous flow of electro-magnetic energy through the poles from the Planetary Ascension Vehicle. <u>You are now prepared to ascend.</u> <u>When Mother Earth shifts, everyone connected to her though their Individual Ascension Vehicles will shift with her.</u>

Chapter Five

General Instructions for the Four Activations

General Instructions for the Four Activations

Just to be clear, the Four Activations are:

1. Fifth Dimension Lightbody Activation

2. Sixth Dimension Activation

3. Seventh Dimension Activation

4. 12-Strand DNA Activation

Have fun with your partner as you do these activations. Don't take it all *too* seriously. After a long and arduous journey through many lifetimes, doing these activations as you prepare for Ascension should be a time of celebration and joy.

Four sessions are needed to complete the Four Activations.

The Activations must be done in the following sequence. That's because we move up through the dimensions in ascending order. For example, we can't just jump in at the Seventh Dimension. Remember, all previous Activations are repeated in each session before the new Activation is added.

First Session:

Fifth Dimension Lightbody Activation

Second Session:

Fifth Dimension Lightbody Activation
Sixth Dimension Activation added

Third Session:

Fifth Dimension Lightbody Activation
Sixth Dimension Activation
Seventh Dimension Activation added

Fourth Session:

Fifth Dimension Lightbody Activation
Sixth Dimension Activation
Seventh Dimension Activation
12-Strand DNA Activation added

Sessions should be spaced from one week apart to one month apart. Some people prefer a very fast pace whereas others are more comfortable with spacing sessions further apart.. Be guided by your personal preference.

Two people are needed to do the activations—the one *giving* the activation and the one *receiving* the activation. **Once the Four Activations are complete, maintenance sessions**

can be done alone. In the instructions, partners are referred to as the Giver and the Receiver. The instructions are written for the Giver, who is the one activating the partner.

It is not necessary to spend a lot of time and effort memorizing what to say and what to do. Follow the step-by-step instructions in the book as you do the activations. This in no way inhibits the energies of the activations. Spirit does not mind that you peek in the book.

Crystals are used in all the activations. Before initial use, the crystals must be programmed. This need be done only once. The instructions for each Activation include a recommended programming meditation for the crystals. You may write something special in your own words if you prefer.

The receiver lies down to receive the Activations. If using a massage table, the surrounding crystals may be placed on stools or chairs. If using a bed, the Receiver should lie across the foot of the bed, so the Giver can easily access the Receiver's head and feet. If the Receiver is too tall and there is no room on the bed for the crystals, then position chairs or stools against the bed near the Receiver's head and feet for the crystals to rest upon. If a sitting position is used, it's a little more difficult to place the crystals in all the right places.

That's not an insurmountable problem, however, because the activation energies don't seem to mind.

Creating a conducive atmosphere during a session through the use of candles, soft music and the like can add to the experience. Discuss preferences with your partner. Otherwise, just follow the directions. The method is very flexible and forgiving of a glitch or bobble here or there.

Chakra locations on the body vary from one spiritual system to another. In this book, chakras are designated with self-identifiable names to eliminate confusion. For example, the location of the *second* chakra may not be clear, but the location of the *navel* chakra is self-evident. Our chakra locations are designated as follows:

7th—Crown Chakra
6th—Third Eye Chakra
5th—Throat Chakra
4th—Heart Chakra
3rd—Solar Plexus Chakra
2nd—Navel Chakra
1st—Sexual Chakra

At the beginning of the session, make sure your partner is comfortable and relaxed. Use a pillow and blanket if desired.

At the end of the session, allow your partner to rest in silence for a brief time, then end the session with a blessing such as this one. Say: “Let us end this session with a blessing just for you:

‘Peace for the Soul,
Joy for the Spirit,
Love for the heart;
May these blessings be yours,
Today and every day,
Amen, amen, amen’”

Chapter Six

Instructions for the Fifth Dimension Lightbody Activation

Instructions for the Fifth Dimension Lightbody Activation

Getting Ready for the First Activation

Crystals Needed.

A piece of amethyst geode or a clear quartz crystal is commonly used for Pele, the Hawaiian Goddess of Fire. A green crystal, fluorite or aventurine, works well for Sea Turtle. Pink rose quartz crystals are inexpensive and widely available making them a popular choice for Dolphin. If you already have other favorite crystals, by all means use them. The above suggestions are only guide lines. Just be sure that you choose actual crystals that are not just pebbles. Once programmed, use them only for activations.

Programming the Crystals.

Hold crystal in your hand as you say for Pele "By the power vested in me through Spirit, I bless this crystal with the energy of Pele." For Sea Turtle: "By the power vested in me through Spirit, I bless this crystal with the energy of Sea Turtle."

For Dolphin: "By the power vested in me through Spirit, I bless this crystal with the energy of Dolphin."

The Crystal Layout. Triangular shape. See *Figure 6-1*.

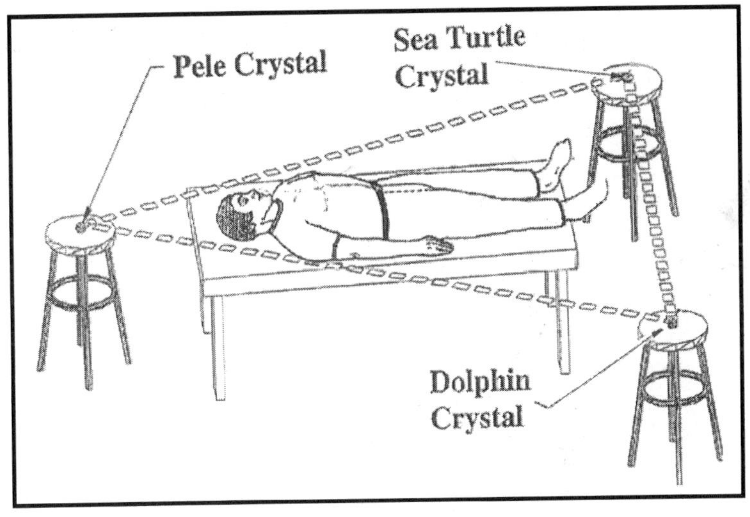

Figure 6-1 – Crystal Layout for Fifth Dimension Activation

The Steps in the Fifth Dimension Lightbody Activation

1 – Open Eighth Chakra

2 – Braid Upper Chakras

3 – Braid Lower Chakras

4 – Open the Heart

5 – Cocoon the Body

6 – Activate Core of Light

7 – Activate Cylinders of Light

8 – Activate Prana Flow

9 – Activate Cellular Awareness

Step 1 – Open Eighth Chakra

To begin, you say, "Now I am going to open the Eighth Chakra located beyond your Crown Chakra."

Instruct your partner to repeat after you the following affirmation, one sentence at a time, saying the affirmation three times in all:

Say, "Repeat after me:"

"I am the Light of the world." (Partner repeats.)

"I am the Light of the world." (Partner repeats.)

"I am the Light of the world." (Partner repeats.)

Simultaneously move the flat of your hand several times back and forth through the Eighth Chakra located beyond the Crown Chakra. See *Figure 6-2*.

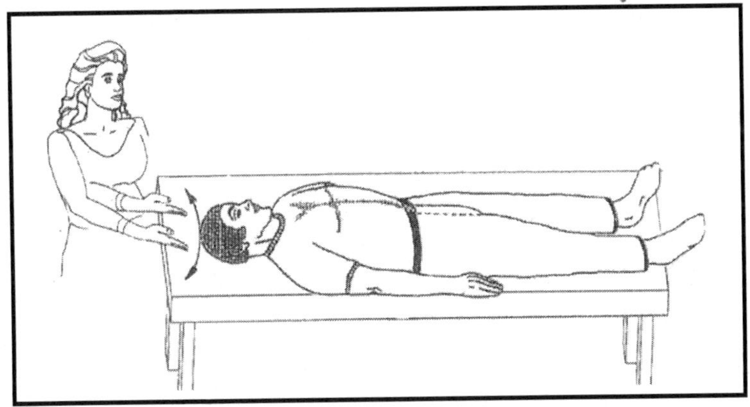

Figure 6-2 – Open Eighth Chakra

Step 2 – Braid Upper Chakras

Say, "Now I am running a strand of light from your Crown Chakra to your heart."

With your fingers, pinch and pull an imaginary strand out of the Crown Chakra and lay it on the Heart Chakra. Use hand motions in the direction of the arrows. These energy strands are called aka cords in the Hawaiian Huna tradition. *See Figure 6-3.*

Now say, "I am running a strand of light from your Third Eye to your heart."

Grasp an energy strand and pull it from the Third Eye and lay it over the heart.

Say, "Now I am running a strand of light from your throat chakra to your heart."

Grasp an energy strand and pull it from the throat chakra and lay it over the heart.

Say, "Now I am braiding the three strands together."

Using both hands, move your fingers to simulate braiding. Start at the chest and braid upward about twelve inches. Repeat three times. Lay braid over heart. With intent and imagination, “see” these very real strands of light.

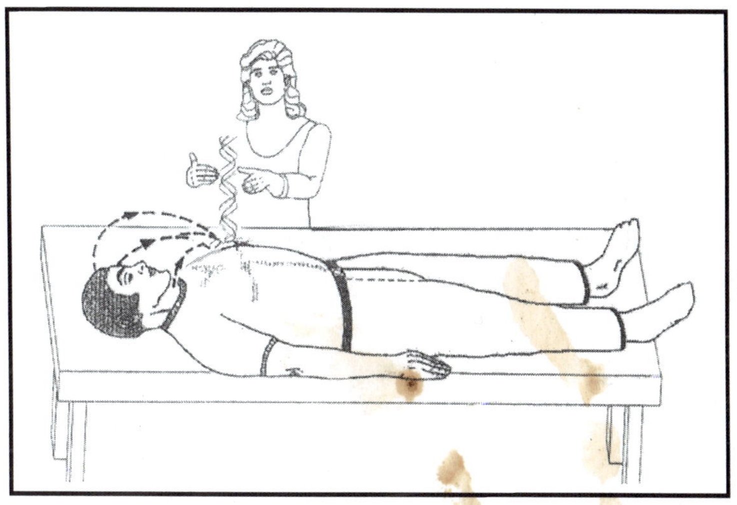

Figure 6-3 – Braid Upper Chakras

Step 3 – Braid Lower Chakras

Say, "Now I am running a strand of light from your Sexual Chakra to your heart."

Repeat the method used for running the strands of light in the upper chakras by moving your hands in the direction of the arrows. *See Figure 6-4.*

Say, "Now I am running a strand of light from the Navel Chakra to the heart."

Say, "Now I am running a strand of light from the Solar Plexus Chakra to the heart."

Say, "Now I am braiding the three stands together."

Braid the three strands together three times as you did for the upper chakras.

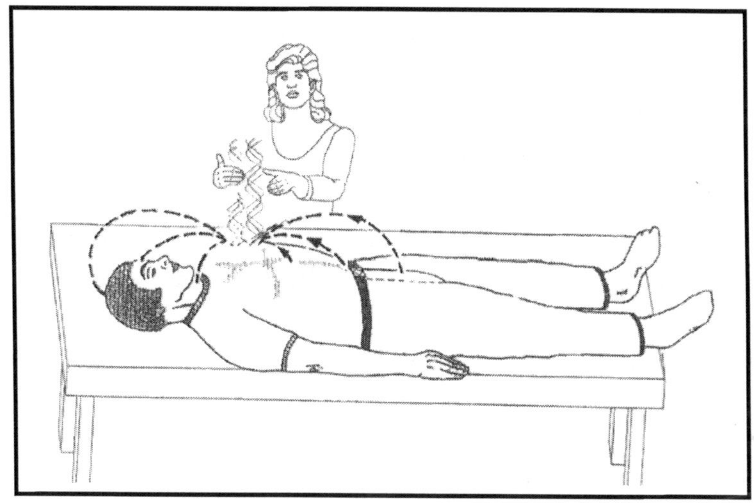

Figure 6-4 – Braid Lower Chakras

Step 4 – Open the Heart

Say, "I first pull a strand from the heart chakra and then braid it together with the upper chakra and lower chakra braids to form one large braid. Now the energy from all your chakras is flowing out of your heart."

Encourage the flow to burst forth by repeatedly moving your hands away from the heart. This step is most important. An open, flowing heart feeds the activation process. *See Figure 6-5.*

Say, "Your heart is open and a spiral of energy is pouring out."

Let the energy flow out of the heart for a minute or two before moving on.

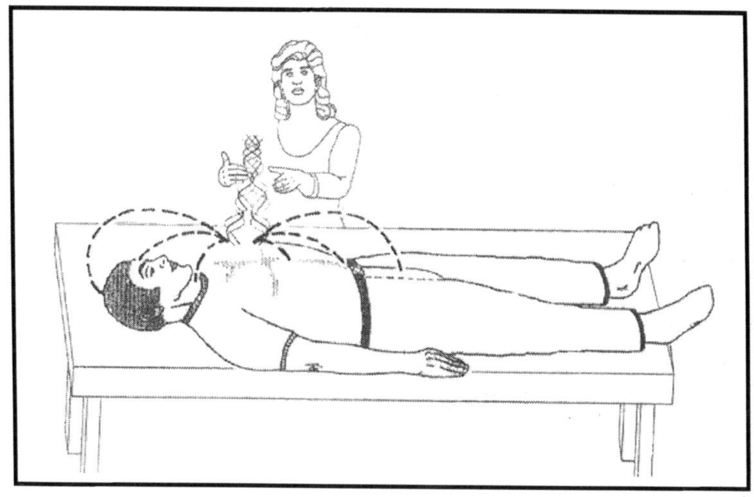

Figure 6-5 – Open the Heart

Step 5 – Cocoon the Body

Say, "Now I am going to cocoon your body in your own love energy. I am taking hold of the spiral of energy flowing from your heart and wrapping it around you. Around and around."

With your arms extended, inscribe a large horizontal oval as you imagine your partner being wrapped in a cocoon surrounding the entire body. Repeat the movement about a dozen times to make sure the cocoon is well in place. *See Figure 6-6.*

Now say, "You are floating in a cocoon of your own love energy. Floating, floating, floating. You are safe. You are secure. You are surrounded by the love energy flowing out of your own heart."

Allow your partner a minute or two to float in this loving cocoon energy. Remember to take your time – do not rush doing the steps in the activations.

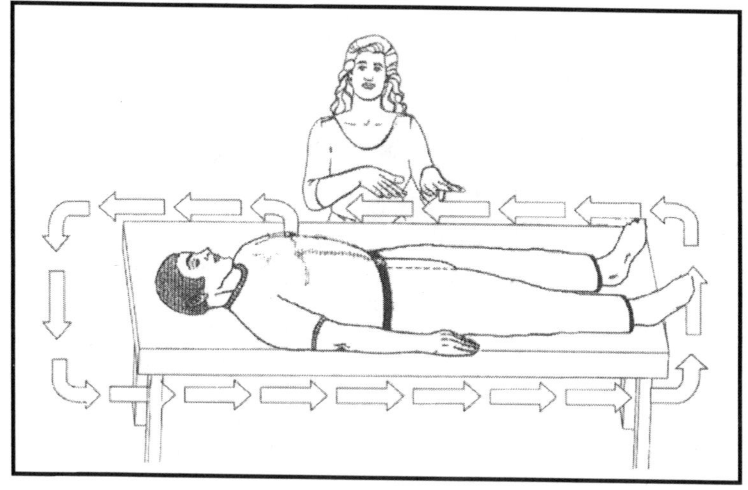

Figure 6-6 – Cocoon the Body

Step 6 – Activate Core of Light

Say, "Now I am inserting a Core of Light about three inches in diameter into your Crown Chakra and down through the center of your body, out your Sexual Chakra and down, down, down below your feet."

To move this fluorescent-like tube through the body, lay the flat of your hand against the top of the head. Now slowly walk toward the feet. With one finger, touch the body lightly at several points as you go – throat, chest, abdomen, knees and ankles.

Say, "The Core of Light now extends through the axis of your body."

Return to the head and look toward the Receiver's feet. *See Figure 6-7.*

Say, "I am now rotating the Core of Light counter-clockwise faster and faster toward the speed of light. Spinning, spinning, faster and faster. This activates your Fifth Dimension physical body cells by spinning light into the cells and raising their vibration.

Imagine you are rotating the Core of Light in a COUNTER-CLOCKWISE direction as you face the top of your partner's head. Move your hands faster and faster in a large circular motion. This spinning Core of Light moves the physical body up into the lightbody vibration.

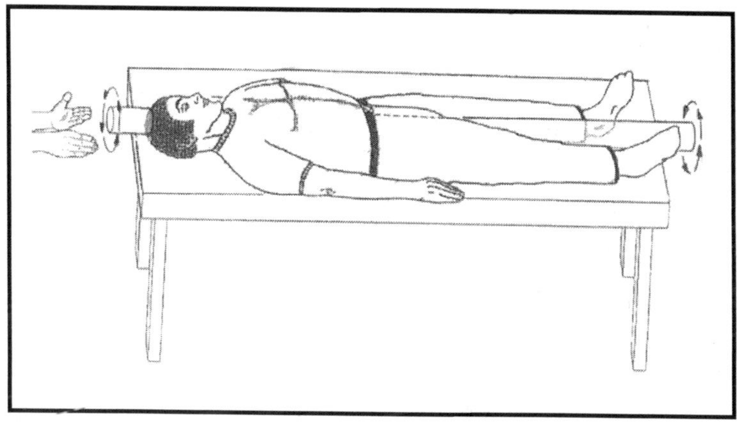

Figure 6-7 – Activate Core of Light

Step 7 – Activate Cylinders of Light

Say, "Now I'm going to encase your body from head to toe inside a Cylinder of Light."

Position your slightly bent arms over the body as though hugging a round cylinder or barrel. Now use short pulling motions and imagine drawing the cylinder down as you go all the way to the feet. The cylinders expand outward as they spin. *See Figure 6-8.*

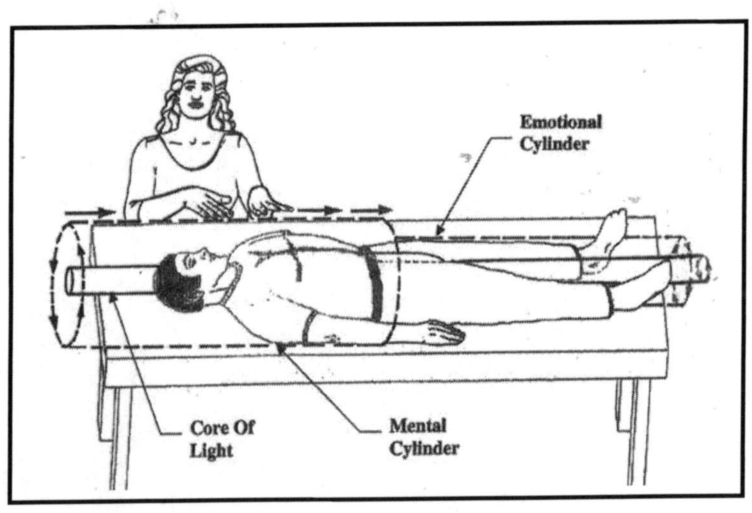

Figure 6-8 – Activate Cylinders of Light

Return to the head of the table (not the side), facing the feet.

Say, "I am spinning the first cylinder clockwise faster and faster toward the speed of light. Spinning, spinning, faster and faster.

Make spinning motions CLOCKWISE with your hands. Imagine turning a big barrel – *and do it with enthusiasm.*

Say, "This activates your Fifth-Dimension emotional body."

Say, "Now I am encasing your body in the second Cylinder of Light surrounding the first cylinder."

Starting at the head, repeat the encasing process as you did with the first cylinder. Return to the head and rotate this second cylinder COUNTER-CLOCKWISE.

Say, "I am spinning the second cylinder faster and faster toward the speed of light. Spinning, spinning, faster and faster"

Say, "This activates your Fifth-Dimension mental body."

Say, "Now I am encasing your body in a third cylinder that slips over the other two."

Starting at the head, repeat the encasing process as you did with the other cylinders. Return to the head and rotate this third cylinder CLOCKWISE.

Say, "I am spinning the third cylinder faster and faster toward the speed of light. Spinning, spinning, faster and faster."

Say, "This activates your Fifth-Dimension spiritual body."

Step 8 – Activate Prana Flow

Say, "Now I am opening the Crown Chakra so prana can flow into your entire body and into all the cells. This is Fifth Dimension energy. You can live on this. Tell your cells that prana is their friend. It is light-food for the cells.

Trace out figure-eight motions horizontally over the length of your partner's body. Do this repeatedly about a dozen times. *See Figure 6-9.*

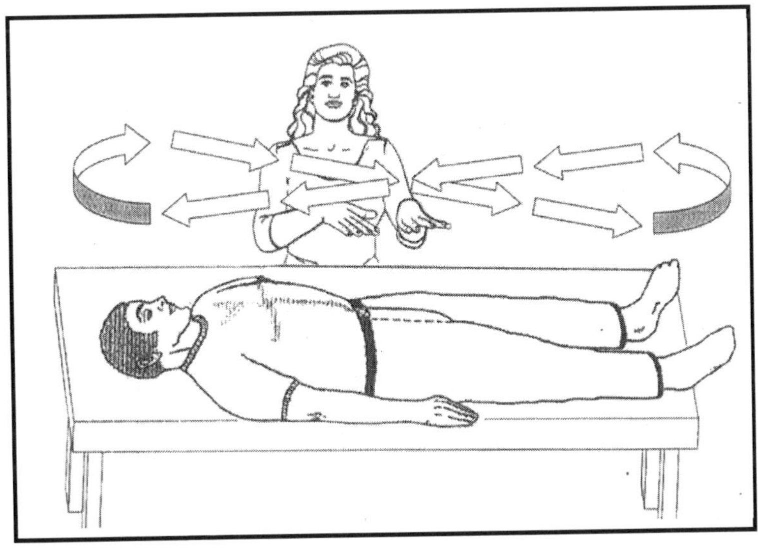

Figure 6-9. Activate Prana Flow

Step 9 – Activate Cellular Awareness

Throughout this step, stand beside your partner and tap, tap, tap *lightly* on the Third Eye with one finger. About two taps per second.
See Figure 6-10.

Say, "Repeat after me:"

"I am the conscious master of the cells in my body." (Partner repeats.)

"I am the conscious master of the cells in my body." (Partner repeats.)

"I am the conscious master of the cells in my body." (Partner repeats.)

Now say, "Repeat after me:"

"I choose peace, joy and harmony for every cell in my body." (Partner repeats.)

"I choose peace, joy and harmony for every cell in my body." (Partner repeats.)

"I choose peace, joy and harmony for every cell in my body." (Partner repeats.)

Now say, "And so it is." (Partner repeats.)

This step activates and awakens the body cells to the wisdom and knowledge of the higher dimensions.

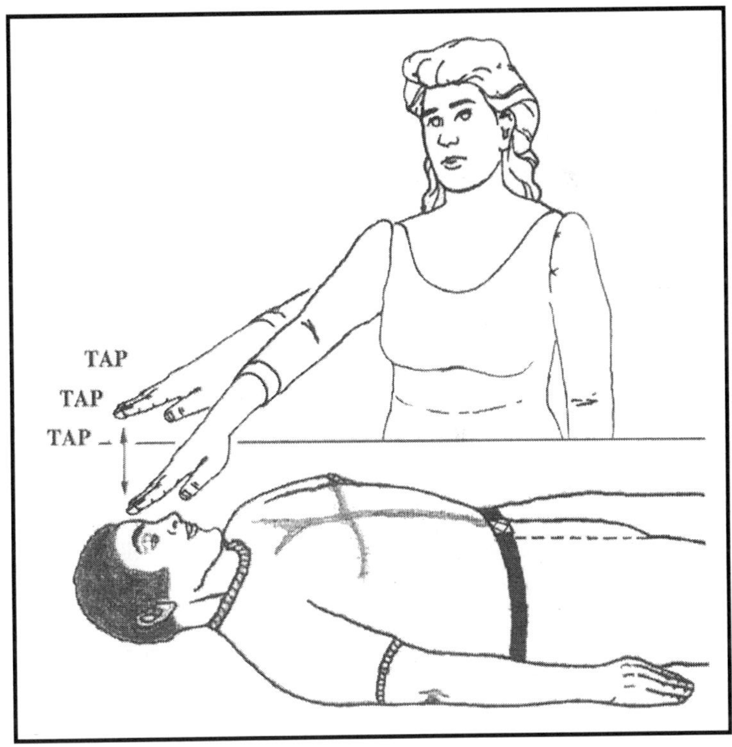

Figure 6-10 – Activate Cellular Awareness

Chapter Seven

Instructions for the Sixth Dimension Activation

Instructions for the Sixth Dimension Activation

Crystals Needed.

Four crystals are needed, two amethyst and two obsidian.

Programming the Crystals.

Hold an amethyst crystal in each hand as you say, "By the power vested in me through Spirit, I program these crystals with the energy of the Divine Feminine."

Hold an obsidian crystal in each hand and say, "By the power vested in me through Spirit, I program these crystals with the energy of the Divine Masculine."

The Crystal Layout.

Place crystals at North, South, East and West Poles after Receiver lies down. *See Figure 7-1.*

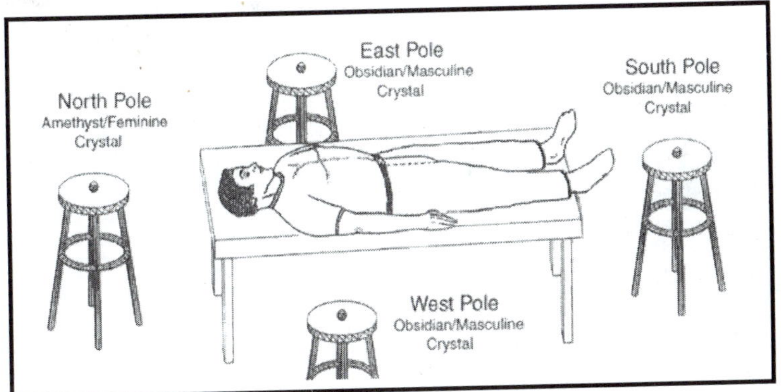

Figure 7-1 – Crystal Layout for Sixth Dimension Activation

The Steps in the Sixth Dimension Activation

1 – Form a Laser Beam Cross on the Body

2 – Activate Heart Chakra

3 – Lower Cross and Activate Sexual Chakra

4 – Raise Cross and Activate Navel Chakra

5 -- Raise Cross and Activate Solar Plexus Chakra

6 – Raise Cross and Activate Throat Chakra

7 – Raise Cross and Activate Third Eye Chakra

8 – Raise Cross and Activate Crown Chakra

9 – Raise Cross and Activate Eighth Chakra

10 – Raise Cross and Activate Metatron Chakras

Step 1 – Form a Laser Beam Cross of Light on the Body

To begin, say, "A feminine crystal is placed beyond your head at the North Pole. A masculine crystal is placed beyond your feet at the South Pole. A feminine crystal is placed at your left side in line with your chest at the East Pole. A masculine crystal is placed at your right side in line with your chest at the West Pole."

Say, "With a laser beam of light, connect the North Pole crystal beyond your head with the South Pole crystal below your feet. See the laser beam right down the center of your body, right on the surface."

With your finger, trace a laser beam line down center of body connecting North and South Pole; then trace a laser beam line across chest connecting East and West Pole. *See Figure7-2.*

Say, "With another laser beam of light right across your chest, connect the East Pole crystal on your left with the West Pole crystal on your right. See the laser beam right across your chest, right on the surface. <u>This forms a laser beam cross on the surface of your body with the</u>

intersection of the cross right on your Heart Chakra."

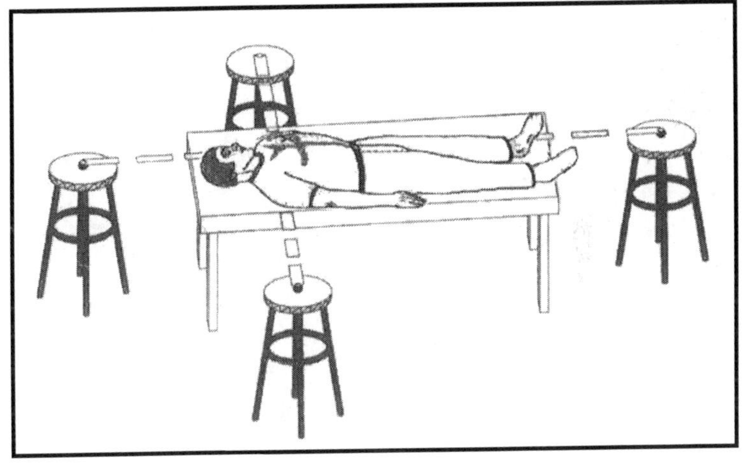

Figure 7-2 – Form a Laser Beam Cross on Body

Step 2 – Activate Heart Chakra

Say, "The intersection point of the cross is a powerful vortex that activates Sixth Dimension energy. As I tap three times, your Heart Chakra activates with Sixth Dimension energy. You are now leaving the Fifth Dimension Realm of Archangel Michael and moving up into the realm of Archangel Metatron, a very high being who sits at the side of the Great Creator."

Activate the Heart Chakra by tapping it three times with the tip of your finger. *See Figure 7-3.*

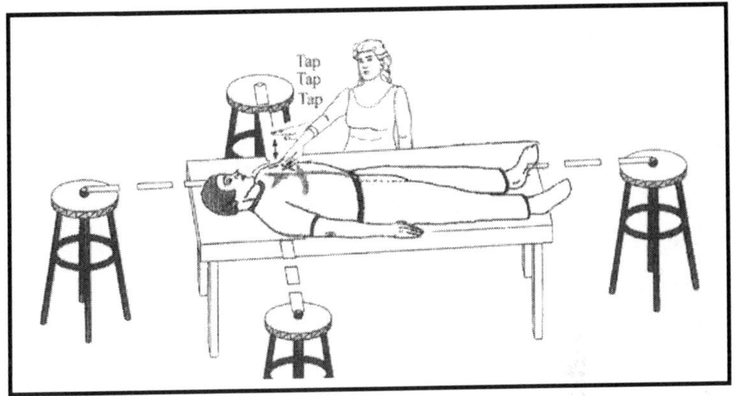

Figure 7-3 – Activate Heart Chakra

Step 3 – Lower Cross and Activate Sexual Chakra

Say, "I can move the cross arm by moving the side crystals, and in that way, reposition the cross on any chakra. I'm now moving the crystals and lowering the cross down to the Sexual Chakra. See it there. As I tap three times, this chakra activates with Sixth Dimension energy.

Move the side crystals in line with the Sexual Chakra and activate by tapping finger in the air above the chakra, respecting the private area of your partner.
See Figure 7-4.

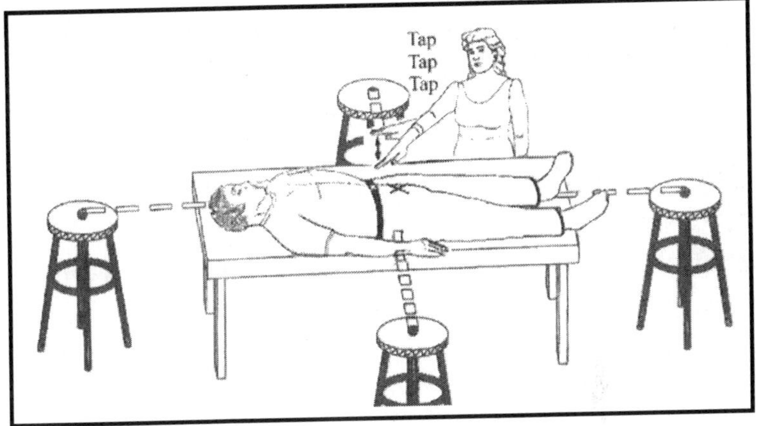

Figure 7-4 – Lower Cross and Activate Sexual Chakra

Step 4 – Raise Cross and Activate Navel Chakra

Say, "Now I'm raising the cross to your Navel Chakra. See it there. As I tap three times, this chakra activates with Sixth Dimension energy."

Move side crystals in line with Navel Chakra and activate by tapping this chakra three times with tip of finger. *See Figure 7-5.*

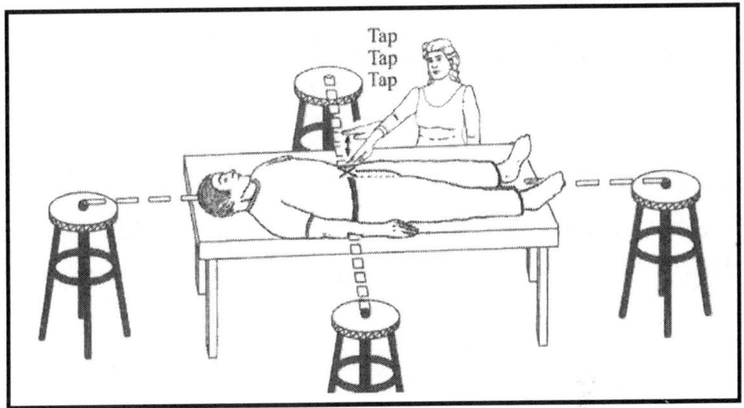

Figure 7-5 – Raise Cross and Activate Navel Chakra

Step 5 – Raise Cross and Activate Solar Plexus Chakra

Say, "Now I'm raising the cross to your Solar Plexus Chakra. See it there. As I tap three times, this chakra activates with Sixth Dimension energy.

Move side crystals in line with the Solar Plexus Chakra and activate it by tapping this chakra three times with the tip of your finger. See *Figure 7-6.*

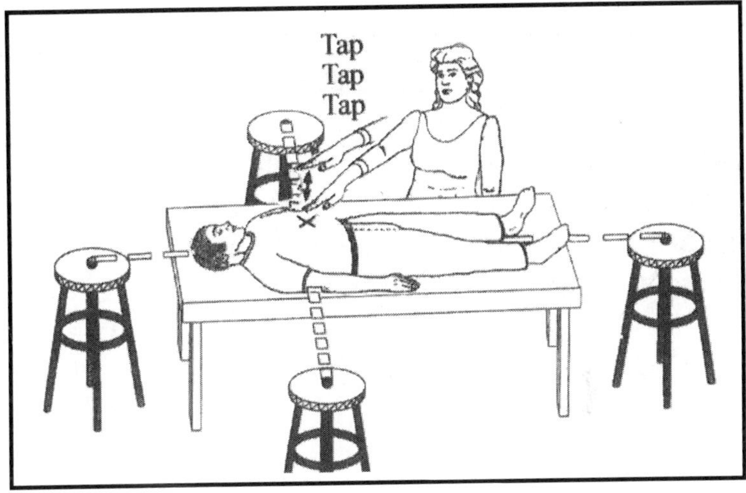

Figure 7-6 – Raise Cross and Activate Solar Plexus Chakra

Step 6 – Raise Cross and Activate Throat Chakra **

Say, "Now I'm raising the cross above the heart (which we've already done) to the Throat Chakra. See it there. As I tap three times, this chakra activates with Sixth Dimension energy."

Move side crystals in line with the Throat Chakra and activate by tapping this chakra three times with the tip of your finger. *See Figure 7-7.*

** A reminder that the heart center is already activated. Proceed from the Solar Plexus to the Throat Center (no need to activate the Heart Center again).

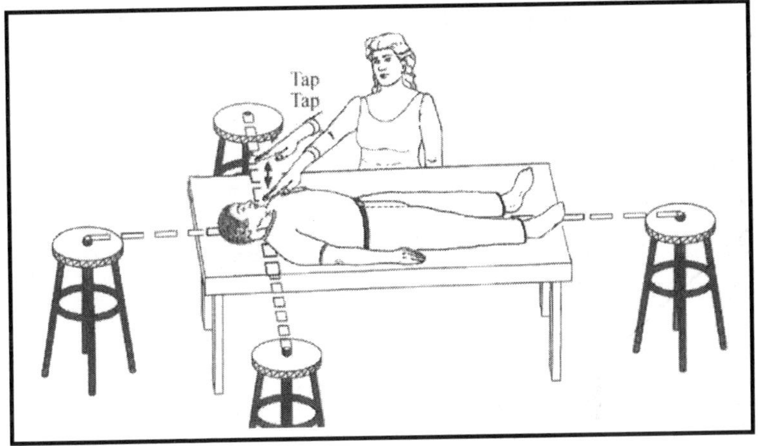

Figure 7-7 – Raise Cross and Activate Throat Chakra

Step 7 – Raise Cross and Activate Third Eye Chakra

Say, "Now I'm raising the cross to the Third Eye Chakra. See it there. As I tap three times, this chakra activates with Sixth Dimension energy."

Move side crystals in line with the Third Eye Chakra and activate it by tapping this chakra three times with the tip of your finger. *See Figure 7-8.*

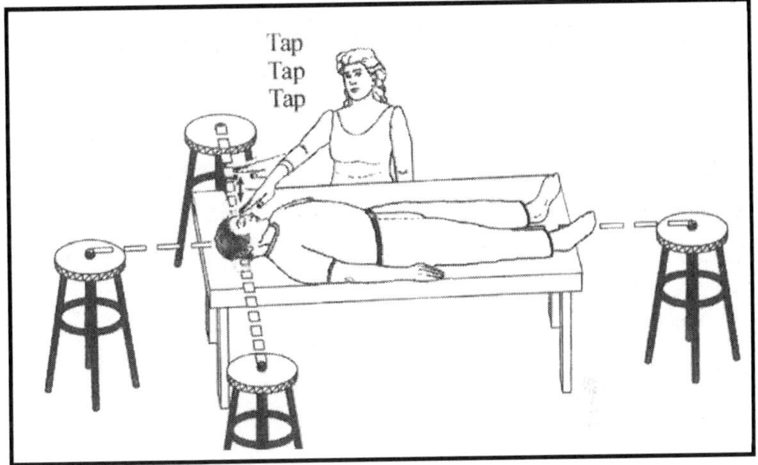

Figure 7-8 –Move Cross and Activate Third Eye Chakra

Step 8 – Move Cross and Activate Crown Chakra

Say, "Now I'm raising the cross to the Crown Chakra. See it there. As I tap three times, this chakra activates with Sixth Dimension energy."

Move side crystals in line with the Crown Chakra and activate it by tapping this chakra three times with the tip of your finger. *See Figure 7-9.*

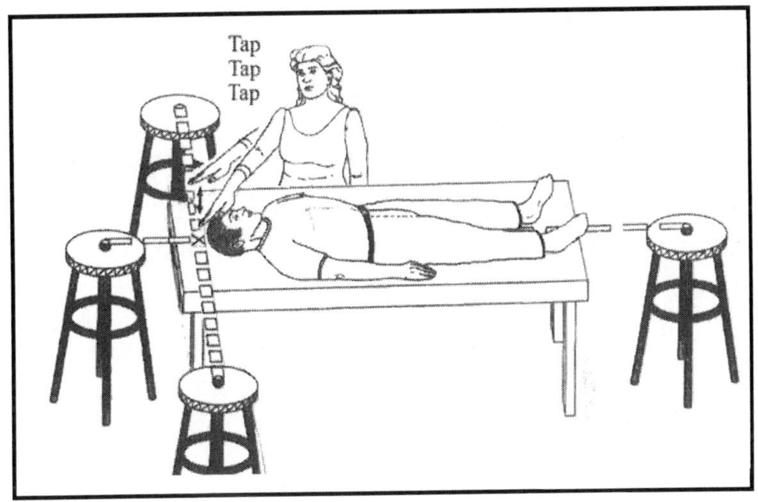

Figure 7-9 – Raise Cross and Activate Crown Chakra

Step 9 – Raise Cross and Activate Eighth Chakra

Say, "Now I'm raising the cross to the Eighth Chakra above the Crown Chakra. See it there. As I move my hand three times through the area, this chakra activates with Sixth Dimension energy.

Move side crystals about a foot above the Crown Chakra and activate the Eighth Chakra by moving your hand three times through this area. *See Figure 7-10.*

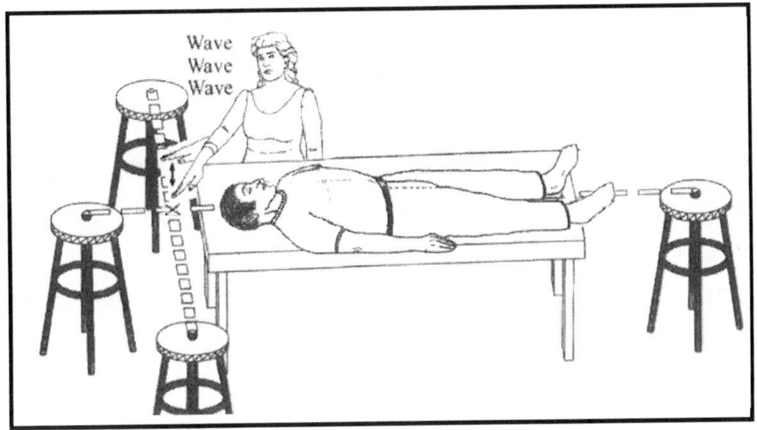

Figure 7-10 – Raise Cross and Activate Eighth Chakra

Step 10 – Raise Cross and Activate Metatron Chakras

Say, "Now I'm raising the cross one last time, to a position above the Eighth Chakra. See it there. As I move my hand three times through the area, Metatron Chakras Nine, Ten and Eleven open simultaneously."

Move side crystals beyond the Eighth Chakra and activate Metatron Chakras Nine, Ten and Eleven by moving your hand three times through this area. These three chakras activate simultaneously. See *Figure 7-11*

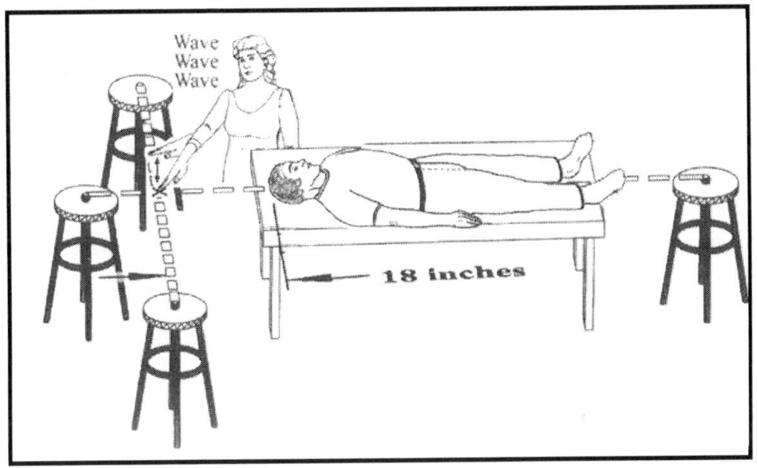

Figure 7-11 – Raise Cross and Activate Metatron Chakras

Chapter Eight

Instructions for the Seventh Dimension Activation

Instructions for the Seventh Dimension Activation

Crystals Needed.

Use the same four crystals as those in the Sixth Dimension Activation.

Programming the Crystals.

It is not necessary to reprogram the crystals.

Crystal Layout.

Because previous activations are always repeated during a session, the Sixth Dimension Activation directly precedes this activation so the North and South crystals are already in place. Move the East and West crystals to once more form a laser beam cross on the heart. Begin the session with crystals in this position. *See Figure 8-1.*

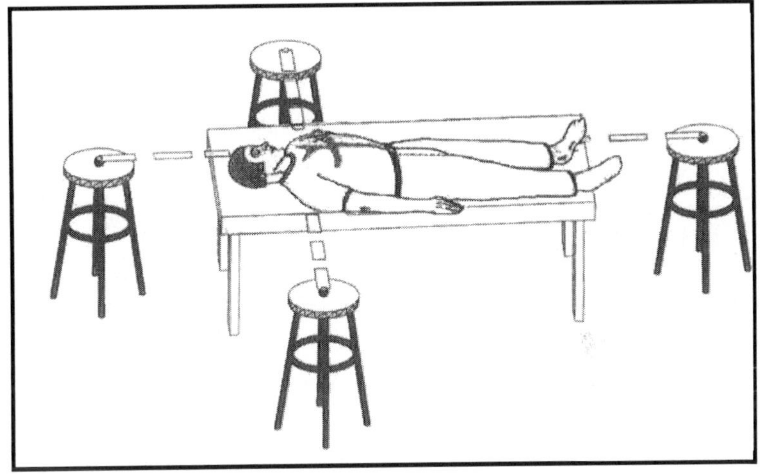

Figure 8-1 – Reposition Cross on Heart Chakra

The Steps in the Seventh Dimension Activation

Step 1 – Move Crystals into Unified Layout

Step 2 – Connect Poles with Laser Beam of Light

Step 3 – Open Poles to Christ Flow

Step 4 – Open Alpha Chakra

Step 5 – Open Omega Chakra

Step 6 – Anchor Christ Cloud for Five Minutes

Step l – Move Crystals into Unified Layout

Say, "We just finished the Sixth Dimension Activation and have repositioned the cross on your Heart Chakra."

Say, "Now we are moving the feminine crystal at the East Pole down to the South Pole alongside the masculine crystal. We are also moving the masculine crystal at the East Pole up to the North Pole alongside the feminine crystal. In this Seventh Dimension, the East and West Poles are absorbed into Oneness by the North and the South Poles.

Move the feminine crystal at the East Pole on the left down to the South Pole below the feet alongside the masculine crystal. Move the masculine crystal at the West Pole on the right side up beyond the head alongside the feminine crystal. *See Figure 8-2.*

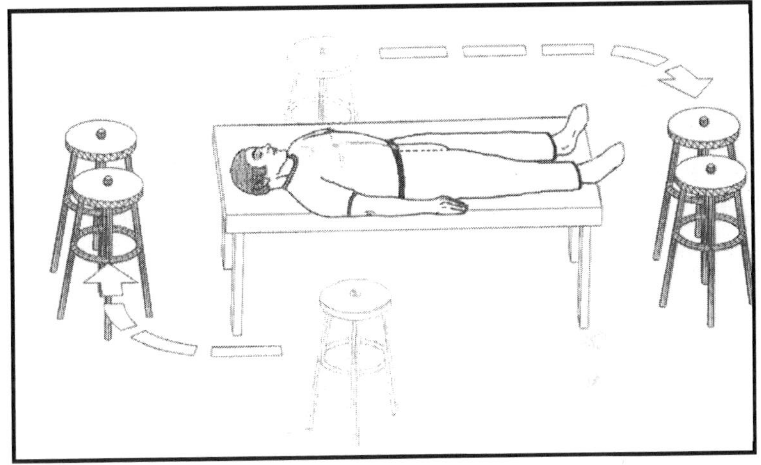

Figure 8-2 – Move Crystals into Unified Layout

Say, "At both the North and South Poles, a feminine and a masculine crystal rest side by side. In the Seventh Dimension, there is no Feminine-Masculine polarity. Therefore, the Feminine-Masculine crystals blend together into Oneness. Now there is only Unity."

Step 2 – Connect Poles with Laser Beam of Light

Say, "With a Laser Beam of Light, connect the Unified North Pole with the Unified South Pole. See the Laser Beam of Light right down the centerline of your body, right on the surface."

Make this connection by standing at the side of the Receiver and moving your body, arm and finger down the centerline of the body, from above the head to below the feet. *See Figure 8-3.*

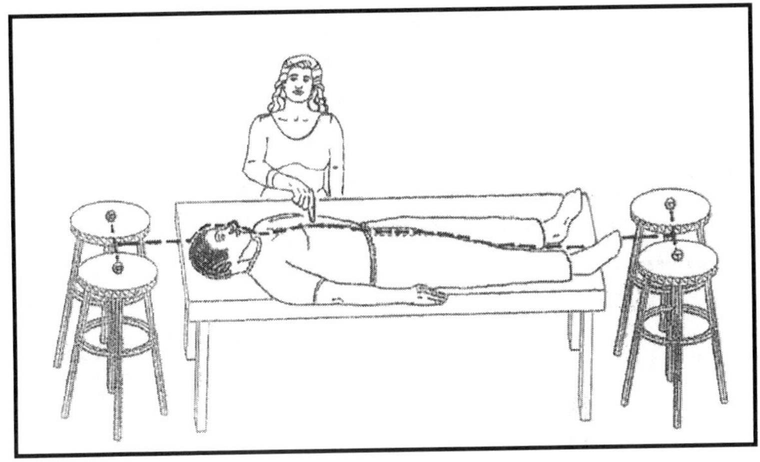

Figure 8-3 – Connect Poles with Laser Beam of Light

Step 3 – Open Poles to Christ Flow

Say, "I'm tapping on your Heart Chakra to open the North and South Poles of your energy field. Tapping, tapping, tapping. Tapping, tapping, tapping."

Positioning yourself at Receiver's side, tap Heart Chakra with the tip of your finger. Do this nine times. *See Figure 8-4.*

Say, "As I tap, the North and South Poles of your energy field open simultaneously and Quantum Christ Energy from the Seventh Dimension flows in, surrounding you in a cloud one hundred feet in diameter. This is a cloud of Oneness. This is a cloud of Unity. This is cloud of Unconditional Love. You are floating in it."

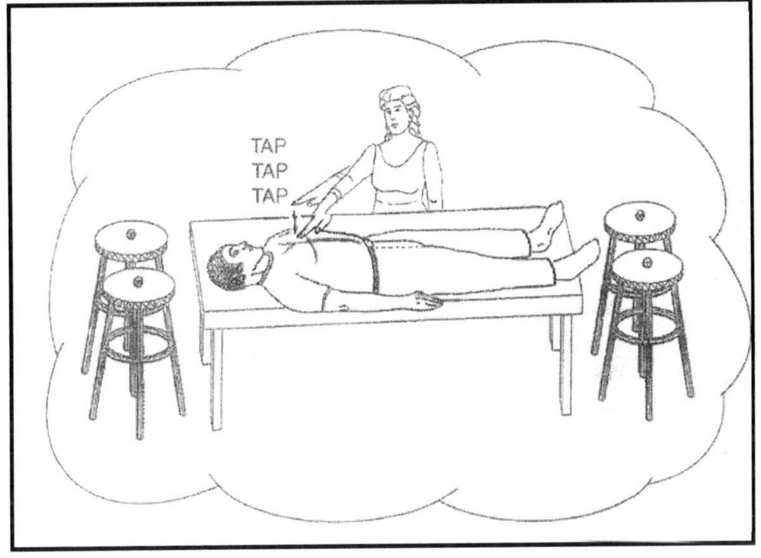

Figure 8-4 – Open Poles to Christ Flow

Step 4 – Open Alpha Chakra

Say, "Now I'm moving my hands through your energy field way out beyond your head. As I do this three times, the twelfth chakra called the Alpha Chakra opens."

Standing three or four feet beyond the partner's head wave your arms and hands in large movements three times through the air, thereby opening the Alpha Chakra way beyond your partner's head. *See Figure 8-5.*

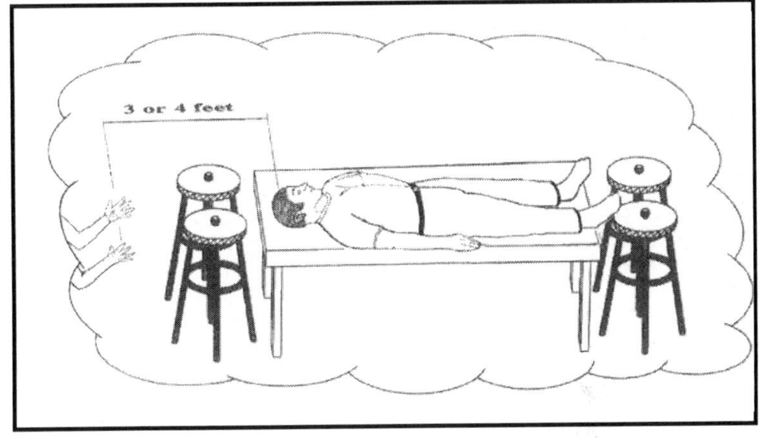

Figure 8-5 – Open Alpha Chakra

Step 5 – Open Omega Chakra

Say, "Now I'm moving my hands through your energy field way out beyond your feet. As I do this three times, your Thirteenth Chakra, called the Omega Chakra, opens.

Standing three or four feet beyond partner's feet, wave your arms and hands in large movements three times through the air, thereby opening the Omega Chakra way beyond your partner's feet. *See Figure 8-6.*

Say, "These last two are Chakras Twelve and Thirteen. In order to ascend, you must be open through the Thirteenth Chakra as you are now."

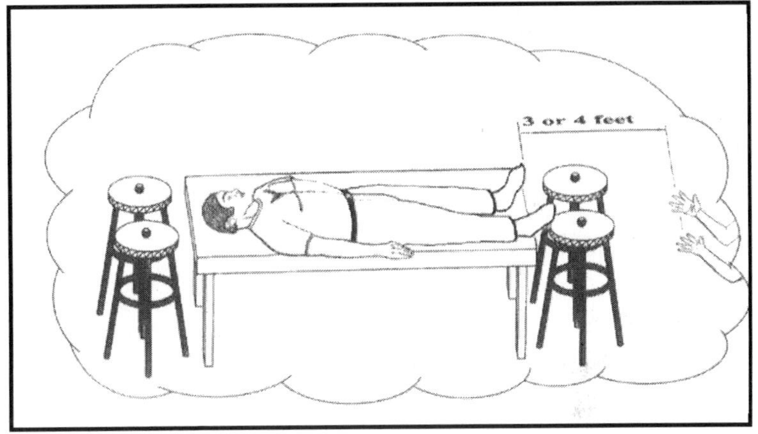

Figure 8-6 – Open Omega Chakra

Step 6 – Anchor Christ Cloud for Five Minutes

Say, "Continue to float in the cloud of Quantum Christ Energy as it anchors around you. Do this for five minutes. Enjoy."

Allow the Receiver to quietly, peacefully and joyfully float in this cloud for five minutes (or longer), anchoring the energy. Be silent and remain in a stationary position.
See Figure 8-7.

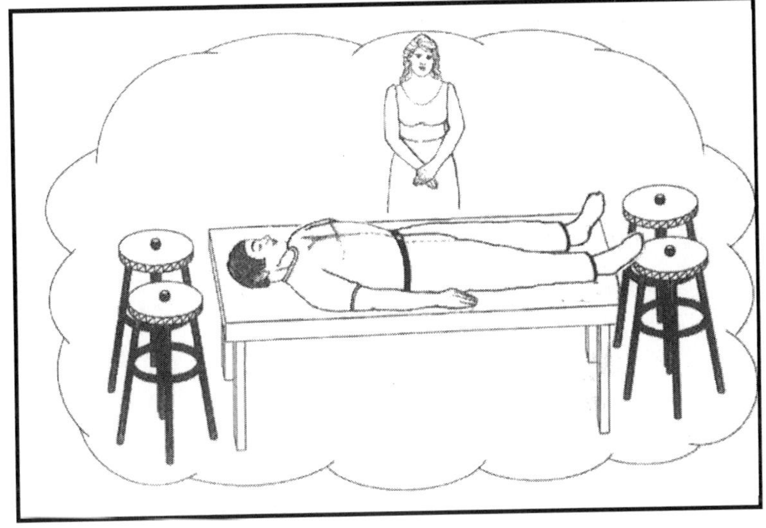

Figure 8-7 – Anchor Christ Cloud for Five Minutes

Chapter Nine

Instructions for the 12-strand DNA Activation

Instructions for the 12-strand DNA Activation

Crystals Needed.

The four crystals used in the previous Seventh Dimension Activation are also used here. In addition, eight small rose quartz crystals (1/2 inch to 1 inch diameter) are needed.

Programming the Crystals.

To program the rose quartz crystals, hold four in each hand and say: "May the power of Spirit flowing through me program these eight crystals to activate the 12-strand DNA in the eight master cells of my body."

The Crystal Layout.

The crystal layout from the Seventh Dimension Activation directly preceding remains in place here. The eight rose quartz crystals are set aside for use during the session. *See Figure 9-1.*

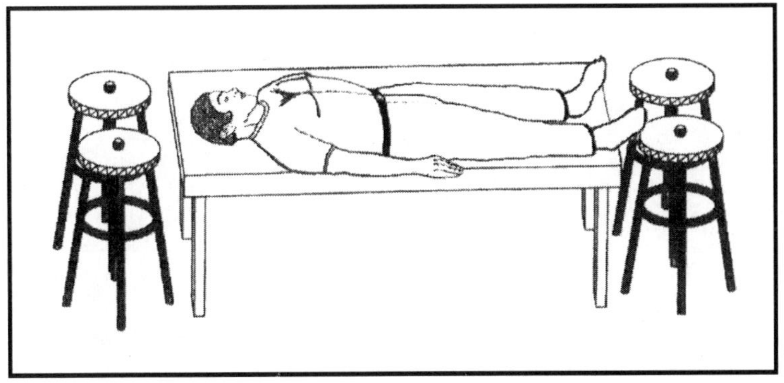

Figure 9-1 – Crystal Layout for 12-strand DNA Activation

The Steps in the 12-strand DNA Activation

Step 1 – Activate First Master Cell

Step 2 – Activate Second Master Cell

Step 3 – Activate Third Master Cell

Step 4 – Activate Fourth Master Cell

Step 5 – Activate Fifth Master Cell

Step 6 – Activate Sixth Master Cell

Step 7 – Activate Seventh Master Cell

Step 8 – Activate Eighth Master Cell

Step 9 – Do "Thymus Thump"

Step 1 – Activate First Master Cell

Say, "You are at the Seventh Dimension quantum level, where matter can be changed by pure intent. Therefore, we can access the eight master cells of your body in the thymus gland and change the DNA from two strands to 12 strands. These master cells will then change all the other cells in the body. To activate each cell, I will place a crystal over the thymus and simulating pulling motions, I will count to 10, pulling out a strand on each count.

Say, "Repeat after me, 'I am activating 12-strand DNA in my first master cell.'" (Partner repeats.)

(Use a bowl to hold the crystals and remove them one at a time. Use an additional bowl, if necessary, to hold the crystals in place on the partner's body.) Place the first rose quartz crystal on the Receiver's body and count aloud from 1 to 10, each time drawing out an additional strand with hand motions. Count and pull with intention. Do not rush. *See Figure 9-2.*

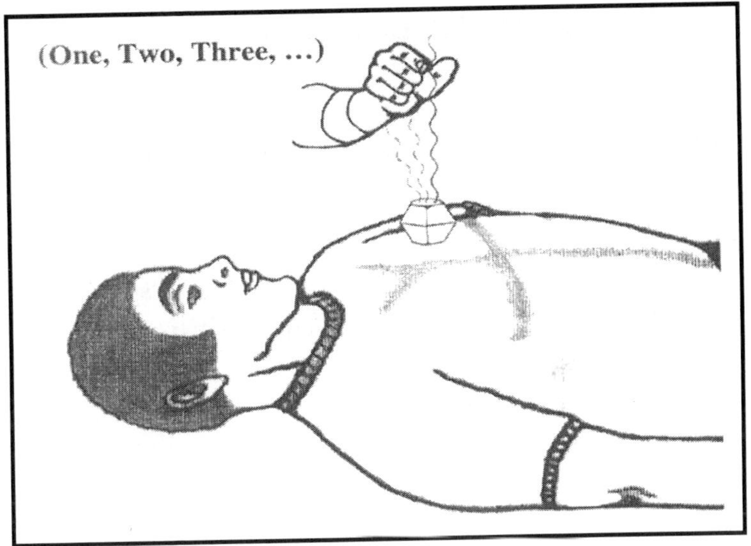

Figure 9-2 – Activate First Master Cell

Step 2 – Activate Second Master Cell

Say, "Repeat after me, 'I am activating the 12-strand DNA in my second master cell.'" (Partner repeats.)

Place the second crystal on the Receiver and count aloud from 1-10, each time pulling an additional strand from the crystal. *See Figure 9-3.*

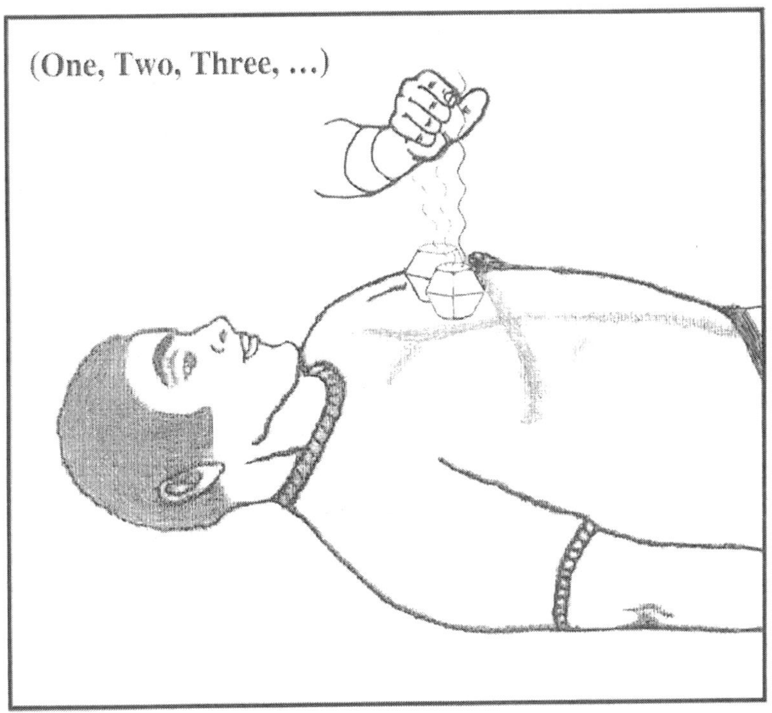

Figure 9-3 – Activate Second Master Cell

Step 3 – Activate Third Master Cell

Say, "Repeat after me, 'I am activating the 12-strand DNA in my third master cell.'" (Partner repeats.)

Place the third crystal on the Receiver and count aloud from 1-10, each time pulling an additional strand from the crystal. *See Figure 9-4*

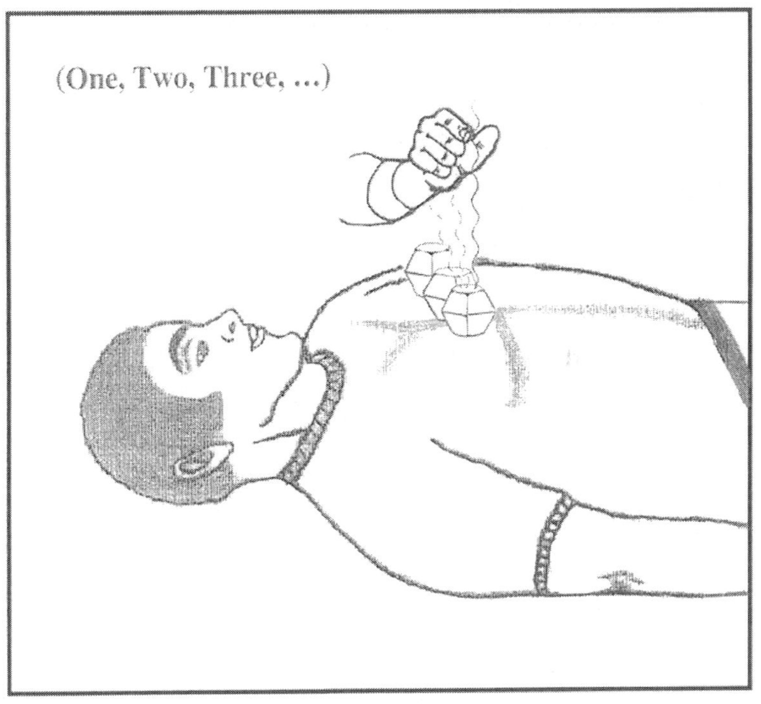

Figure 9-4 – Activate Third Master Cell

Step 4 – Activate Fourth Master Cell

Say, "Repeat after me, 'I am activating the 12-strand DNA in my fourth master cell.'" (Partner repeats.)

Place the fourth crystal on the Receiver and count aloud from 1-10, each time pulling out an additional strand from the crystal. *See Figure 9-5*.

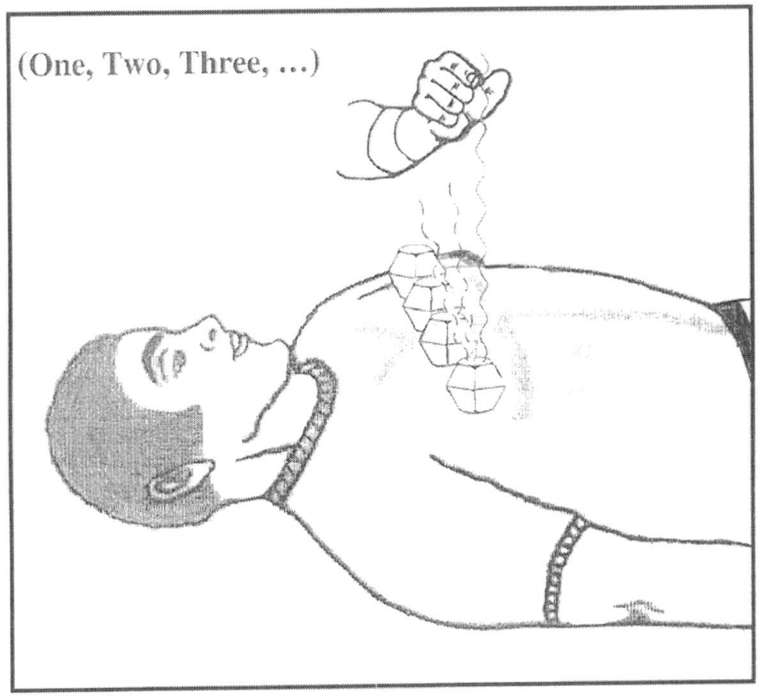

Figure 9-5 – Activate Fourth Master Cell

Step 5 – Activate Fifth Master Cell

Say, "Repeat after me, 'I am activating the 12-strand DNA in my fifth master cell.'" (Partner repeats.)

Place the fifth crystal on the Receiver and count aloud from 1-10, each time pulling an additional strand from the crystal. *See Figure 9-6.*

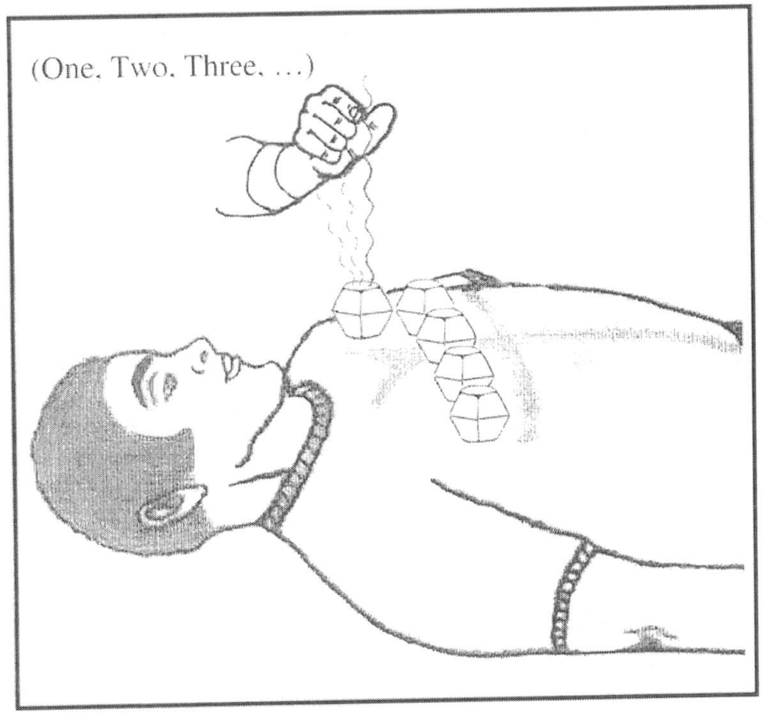

Figure 9-6—Activate Fifth Master Cell

Step 6 – Activate Sixth Master Cell

Now say, "Repeat after me, 'I am activating the 12-strand DNA in my sixth master cell.'" (Partner repeats.)

Place the sixth crystal on the Receiver and count aloud from 1-10, each time pulling an additional strand from the crystal. *See Figure 9-7.*

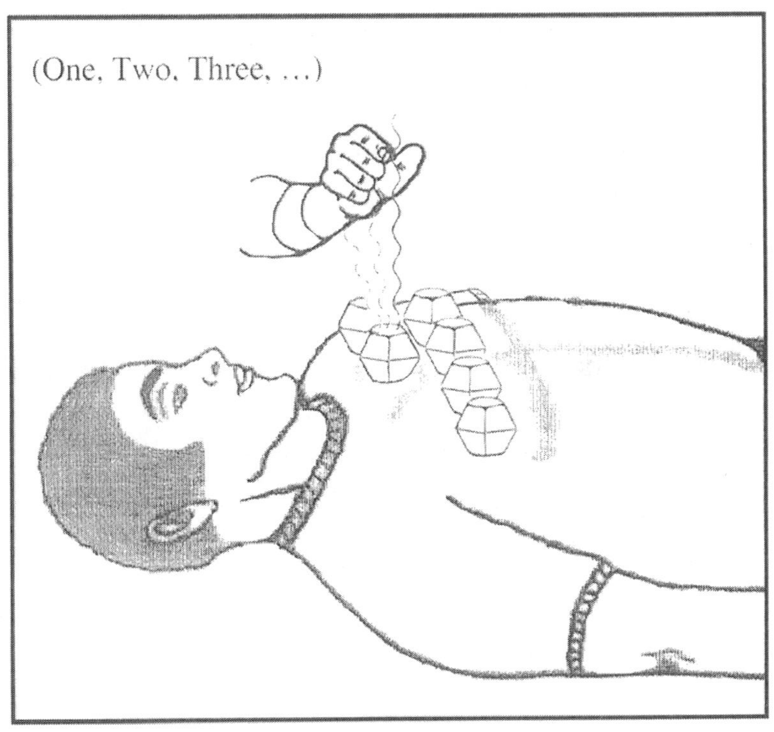

Figure 9-7 – Activate Sixth Master Cell

Step 7 – Activate Seventh Master Cell

Now say, "Repeat after me, 'I am activating the 12-strand DNA in my seventh master cell.'" (Partner repeats.)

Place the seventh crystal on the Receiver and count aloud from 1-10, each time pulling an additional strand from the crystal. *See Figure 9-8.*

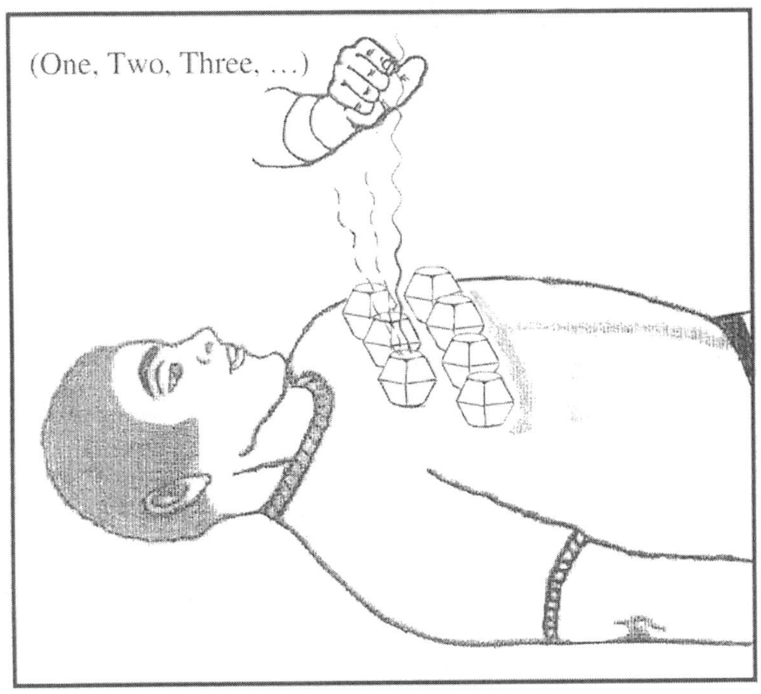

Figure 9-8 – Activate Seventh Master Cell

Step 8 – Activate Eighth Master Cell

Say, "Repeat after me, 'I am activating the 12-strand DNA in my eighth master cell.'" (Partner repeats.)

Place the eighth crystal on the Receiver and count aloud from 1-10, each time pulling an addition strand from the crystal. *See Figure 9-9.*

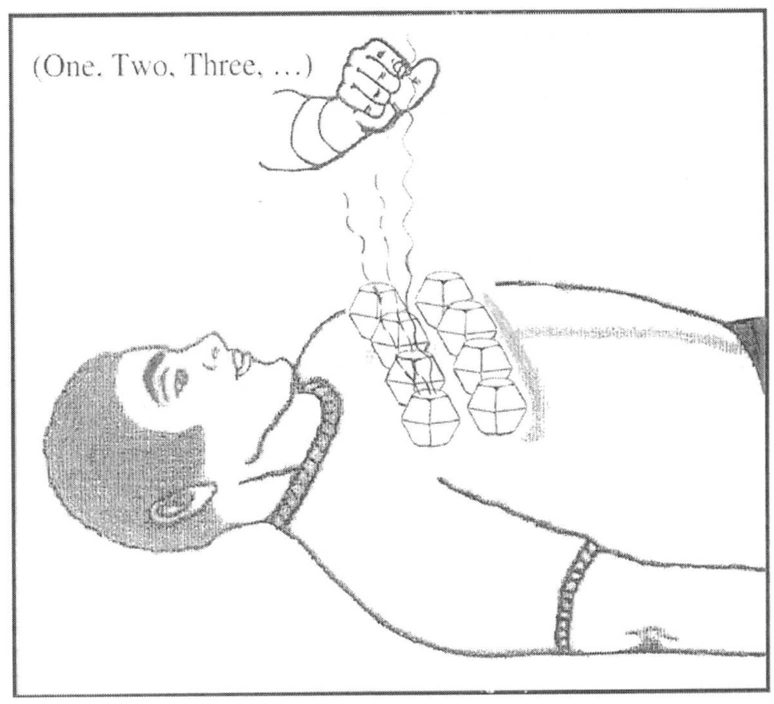

Figure 9-9 – Activate Eighth Master Cell

Step 9 – Do "Thymus Thump"

Say, "As I thump your thymus three times, you may feel a burst of energy spreading throughout your chest, as the additional strands of DNA activate."

Remove the crystals from the body. With your fist, thump the thymus area three times. Do this firmly but not hard enough to hurt. With this thymus thump, the additional DNA strands are off and running. *See Figure 9-10.*

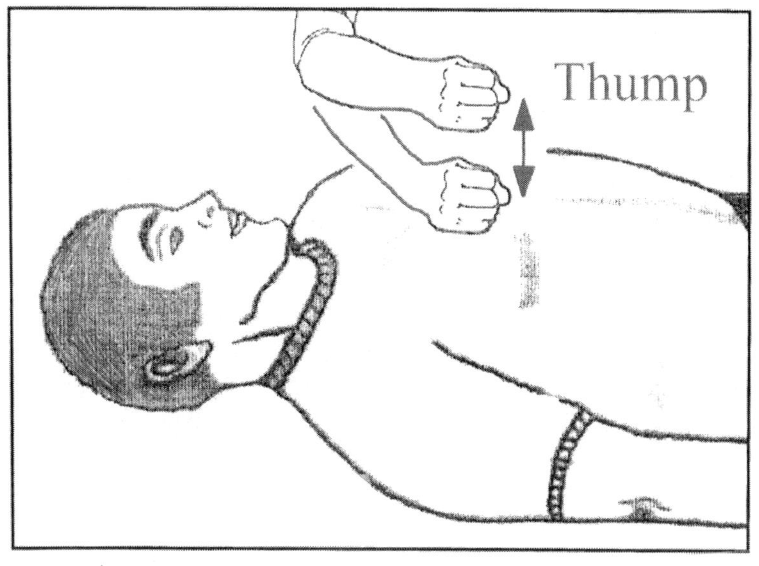

Figure 9-10 – Do Thymus Thump

Chapter 10

How to Keep the Four Activations Going Strong

How to Keep the Four Activations Going Strong

Once the four-session activation process has been completed, you will need a boost on a regular basis in order to keep the Four Activations going strong. That's the way it works here in the density of this dimension. Fortunately, you can do this simply and easily by yourself—no partner needed. However, if you prefer doing this with the help of a partner, by all means do so.

Step One

Set up the Crystal Triangle under your bed and just leave it there. This is the crystal layout used for the Fifth Dimension Lightbody Activation. Looking down from the head of the bed to the foot, the Pelé crystal is positioned at the apex of the triangle underneath your head, the Sea Turtle crystal at the foot of the bed on the left and the Dolphin crystal at the foot of the bed on the right. It is perfectly okay to place the crystals directly on the floor or carpet.

To activate, simply imagine a beam of light from Pelé to Sea Turtle to Dolphin and then back up to Pelé, enclosing yourself in a triangle of light.

Intent is everything! You need do this only once. The energies are now activated and will perform their magic all night, every night while you sleep. For those of you sleeping with partners who have not undergone the activation process, the triangle under the bed will not affect them. If they have undergone the activation process, then they will benefit right along with you.

It's possible to get "wired" from too much energy and that may generate wild dreams at night and feel like you've had too much coffee. If that happens, you need to adjust more gradually by alternating the weeks with the crystal triangle in place. After a month or two, you should be able to set it up full time without feeling over stimulated.

Steps Two, Three and Four need to be done only once a month. These steps are done in sequence, one after the other, and can be completed in about thirty minutes. Considering the critical importance of maintaining the ascension vibration, this is hardly a sacrifice. As a matter of fact, many individuals choose to do this *weekly* simply because the experience is so pleasant and invigorating.

Step Two

Set up the Sixth Dimension Crystal Layout right on the bed using your four crystals. Place a feminine/amethyst crystal beyond your head at the North Pole, a masculine/obsidian crystal beyond your feet at the South Pole, a feminine/amethyst crystal at your left side in line with your chest at the East Pole, a masculine/obsidian crystal at your right side in line with your chest at the West Pole.

Strongly visualizing a laser beam of light, connect North Pole to South Pole and East Pole to West Pole, forming the Cross of Light on the surface of your body, with the intersection of the cross right on your Heart Chakra. This will fully activate Sixth Dimension energy in all of your chakras. With crystals in place, meditate/ relax in this energy for ten minutes.

Step Three

Adjust the crystals into the Seventh Dimension Crystal Layout. Move the feminine crystal at your left side down to the South Pole alongside the masculine crystal. Move the masculine crystal at your right side up to the North Pole alongside the feminine crystal. The feminine-masculine energies at the poles will merge into Oneness. With a laser beam of light down the centerline of your body, right on the surface, connect the Unified North Pole with Unified South Pole. The poles will open and the Quantum Christ Energy from the Seventh Dimension will pour in, surrounding you in a cloud 100 ft. in diameter. Meditate/relax in this energy for ten minutes.

Step Four

You have placed your eight rose quartz DNA crystals inside an appropriate pouch for easy access. Place the pouch with the crystals on your thymus area, i.e., below the throat and above the heart. You are re-stimulating the eight master cells of the body, located in the thymus, to speed the 12-strand DNA Activation through all the cells in your body. Meditate/relax in this energy for ten minutes. (You may extend this time however long you want.)

Congratulations—you did it!

In as little as thirty minutes, you have re-charged your activations for an entire month. Keep up the good work.

Glossary of Terms

Glossary of Terms

2012 (Year)

The end of the present cycle of the Mayan Calendar. The expected date for Earth's and humanity's ascension into the Fifth Dimension.

Activation

An energetic process that prepares one for ascension.

Aka cord

A term from ancient Polynesian shamanism called Huna. It refers to an invisible strand of light capable of carrying a flow of spiritual energy.

Archangel Michael

The archangel who is overseer of the Fifth Dimension.

Archangel Metatron

The archangel who is overseer of the Sixth Dimension. The author's personal guide in the Sixth Dimension.

Ascension

A transformed state characterized by all four bodies–the physical, emotional, mental and spiritual–merging into an integrated whole, capable of transcending the limits of the current dimension and shifting into a higher realm.

Ascension Clearing

Removing the energy blocks in the physical, emotional, mental and spiritual bodies which limit high vibration.

Chakras

Energy centers of the human body system that integrate energy flow among the physical, emotional, mental and spiritual bodies.

Chakra -- Alpha

The 12th chakra located 3 to 4 feet above the physical body (above the head).

Chakra – Omega

The 13th chakra located 3 to 4 feet below the physical body (below the feet).

Chakras – Metatron

Chakras 9, 10 and 11 – all located above the head.

Christ Realm

The Seventh Dimension

Core of Light

A tube of energetic Fifth Dimension light that runs through the internal axis of the body.

Cross of Light

A cross of Sixth Dimension energy used to perform the Sixth Dimension Activation.

Crystal Triangle

A placement of three programmed crystals in a triangular configuration that creates powerful Fifth Dimension energy that will activate your lightbody.

Cylinders of Light

Fifth Dimension cylinders of energy spun around the physical body during the Lightbody Activation process. These cylinders individually activate the emotional, mental and spiritual bodies.

Density

Another term for Dimension.

Dimension

A specific level of consciousness and frequency.

Dimension -- Fourth

The next higher dimension from the Third, still tied to Earth's reincarnation cycles of death and rebirth.

Dimension -- Fifth

The Fifth Dimension–a place of oneness, free of Earth's reincarnation cycles of death and rebirth. This is the dimension we're heading for, the dimension we'll shift into on the scheduled year of 2012, which marks the transition of a long cycle in the famous Mayan Calendar.

Dimension -- Sixth

The dimension above the Fifth - characterized by the energy of compassionate love.

Dimension -- Seventh

The dimension above the Sixth – characterized by the energy of unconditional love – the Christ Realm.

DNA (See also Spiritual DNA)

The double stranded, helical molecular chain found within the nucleus of each cell. DNA carries the total genetic blueprint for growth and reproduction of every cell of the host body. The makeup of any DNA is entirely unique to every being although great similarities exist between members of each species of living organisms.

Dolphin energy

One of the three magical energies of the Crystal Triangle; a high vibration which embodies the spirit of Atlantis; sky energy.

Harmonic Concordance

The date, November 8-9, 2003, was known as Harmonic Concordance and marked the time of an important energy shift for Earth. It is also the date the Pleiadian guides revealed the 12-strand DNA Activation to the author.

Harmonic Convergence

The date, August 17, 1987, was known as Harmonic Convergence and marked the time when earth's probable future shifted from destruction to ascension status.

Huna

A Hawaiian word meaning "the secret or veiled knowledge." A tradition dating back to ancient times and practiced by Kahuna shamans.

Kahuna

A Hawaiian medicine man/woman trained to use the secret knowledge for healing and a number of other beneficial purposes.

Lightbody

The vehicle of ascension. The Fifth Dimension energetic body created by the Activation process and characterized by the cells of the physical body changing from a matter-based form to light-based form. The body's surrounding emotional, mental and spiritual bodies are activated by rapidly spinning cylinders of light surrounding the energetic bodies and expanding to a diameter of about fifty feet.

Master Cells

Energetically (not necessarily medically) it is said that the thymus gland, located in the lower neck area, contains eight master cells which begin the life process by division and contain a master DNA template for cell reproduction throughout the body. After activation, these cells contain the energetic 12-strand DNA expected to impart more extensive human psychic capabilities in the Fifth Dimension.

Merkaba

Another name for lightbody; a Kabbalistic term meaning chariot of ascension.

Metatron Man

The Sixth Dimension aspect of Archangel Metatron. The author's guide in the Sixth Dimension.

Octave

A measure of the vibratory rate change of the physical body. In general, a doubling of frequency. We think of the vibratory rate of the physical body as increasing octave by octave.

Pele energy

One of the magical energies of the Crystal Triangle; the energy of creation itself as symbolized by Pele, the Hawaiian Volcano Goddess.

Pleiadian

A Fifth Dimension entity from a bright seven-star group called the Pleiades (part of the constellation Taurus).

Prana

The pure life force energy called manna in the Christian bible.

Quantum Christ Energy

A description of the energy of the Seventh Dimension.

Sea Turtle energy

One of the magical energies of the Crystal Triangle; a vibration which embodies the spirit of Lemuria; earth energy.

Shaman

Individuals within a community called to their vocation as healer, visionary, messenger and intermediary. They journey into extraordinary states of

consciousness to retrieve soul parts, clear ancestral patterns, exorcise negative energies, interact with animal or nature spirits and other activities that rebalance the psychic and spiritual life of the Collective.

Shamanic Journey

A journey in consciousness to the Underworld, Middle World or Upper World undertaken by a shaman in behalf of another individual or community for the purpose of performing a healing or guidance of some sort.

Soul Retrieval

A special shamanic journey undertaken for the express purpose of returning to the whole any fragmented parts of the psyche that were wounded and separated. A high form of spiritual healing.

Spiritual DNA

Refers to DNA strands which are energetic and not visible to a microscope.

Thymus (Gland)

Medically the thymus gland is source for "T cells" and "killer cells" vital to the body's immune system. Energetically it is

said to contain the 8 master cells which begin the life process by division and as a DNA template for cells throughout the body. Located in the lower neck area and above the heart, it is sometimes called the high heart.

Thymus Thump

Tapping on the thymus area of the chest as part of the 12-strand DNA Activation.

Twelve Strand DNA

Energetic DNA containing 12 strands expected to expand human capabilities in the Fifth Dimension beyond our present 2-strand DNA. Activating this 12-strand energetic DNA is part of the ascension process.

Author's Biography

About Duane Henkle

About Duane Henkle

Duane Henkle

Well into his forties, Duane led the life of a successful corporate manager, suburbanite, husband, father, church leader, scout leader and weekend golfer. Then Duane experienced a vision that revealed his future self as a spiritual teacher who would tap into the power of crystal energy for the purpose of transforming human consciousness.

In pursuit of this vision, he moved from the suburbs of the Midwest to Santa Fe, New Mexico, and then on to Hawaii. It was while living on the Big Island in 1997 that Duane formed a strong psychic connection with a small group of Pleiadian beings who began teaching him – in their words – "the Four Energy Activations that prepare Earth Beings for the coming shift to the Fifth Dimension in 2012." True to the vision years earlier, each of the activations is powered by a crystal layout placed around the body. From that time forward, Duane has devoted his life to receiving this higher Pleiadian knowledge and sharing it with others, so that all with eyes to see and ears to hear can prepare for ascension.

Duane's first book, *The Lightbody Activation Manual*, was published in 2002. He is the co-author, along with his shaman sister Diana Stone. He is the sole author of this writing, *The Ascension Guidebook.*

Duane currently lives in Vancouver, Washington, where he has a busy practice doing energy healing and the Four Activations described in this book. In addition to seeing clients personally, his network of telephone clients stretches across the United States and into other countries as well.

Duane has lectured across the country, including Southwestern College in his former hometown of Santa Fe, New Mexico. He was the keynote speaker at the International Huna Conventions in 2003 and also in 2004.

Information About Duane Henkle's Work

Information about Duane Henkle's Work

Duane Henkle has a busy practice leading clients through the Four Energy Activations described in this book. This work is combined with a powerful form of energy healing that Duane describes as Ascension Clearing. Duane's psychic abilities allow him to see and clear energy blocks in the physical, emotional, mental and spiritual bodies. These blocks are often the result of traumas experienced in past lives. Once eliminated, clients can more easily hold the higher vibrations associated with ascension—hence the term Ascension Clearing. Duane considers Ascension Clearing every bit as important as the activations themselves.

Duane has an extensive international telephone clientele in addition to in-person clients. Using the Chakra Merger Technique learned from his Pleiadian guides, Duane is able to connect long-distance with clients as powerfully as in person. Clients who have experienced both vouch for the fact that Duane's telephone sessions are every bit as energetic, joyful and effective as those conducted in person.

Personalized telephone sessions may include any or all of the following:

1) Crystal Triangle Lightbody Activation –. preparing the client for the coming shift to the Fifth Dimension on 2012. The lightbody is the vehicle that carries us into this New Reality.

2) Crystal Triangle Healing – "seeing" and removing the energy blocks that inhibit lightbody activation, whether from this life or lives past. This work also includes severing cords and connections from unwanted energies and entities.

3) Sixth Dimension, Seventh Dimension and 12-Strand DNA Activations – activating 12-strand DNA in the eight basic cells of the body triggers the energetic transformation of all the body cells to 12-strand DNA. These Activations are the subject of this book and include raising the client's energy field to the Sixth and Seventh Dimensions in preparation for ascension.

4) Heart Activations – Pleiadian guides have shown Duane the beginnings of powerful additional heart-based healing techniques.

These techniques, not yet fully revealed or ready for publication, may be available for sessions with Duane in person or by phone.

To make an appointment for a telephone session, contact Duane by e-mail or by telephone.

Duane's telephone sessions are one hour in duration. Duane makes the phone call and pays for it. During the entire session, Duane and the client converse as Duane facilitates the activation and/or healing process. The session fee is $100 by VISA, MC or check payable to Duane Henkle and mailed to this address:

Duane Henkle
2406 NE 139th St. #221
Vancouver, WA 98686-2768

Telephone number: (360) 571-5748
Cell: (505) 699-3433
E-mail address: duane@cybermesa.com

NOTE: Check with Web site for possible phone or address changes or fee changes

E-mail to sign up for Duane's Free Newsletter
and
Visit his Web site at www.duanehenkle.com

Testimonials About Duane Henkle's Work

Testimonials About Duane Henkle's Work

Testimonial from D. C.

"About two and a half years ago, I asked Duane Henkle to do for me the series of Lightbody Activations he and Diana Stone describe in their book, *The Lightbody Activation Manual*. I wasn't entirely certain about the earth's dimensional shift they and so many others were talking about nor was I sure that the year 2012 was when it would occur, but if it did happen, I certainly didn't want to be left behind! So I decided to go ahead and have it done, just as travel insurance. In the series of ten sessions that followed, Duane not only activated my lightbody and initiated me into the Fifth through the Seventh Dimensions, he also resolved some long-standing difficulties, introduced me to some amazing beings, and opened up some important new directions in my work.

"The first (and to me the most miraculous) result was unexpected—not part of the advertised package! My energy field had gotten quite badly damaged over the years as I went through a very serious car accident and three major surgeries, and as a result I was extremely vulnerable to being swamped psychically in client work. I was also plagued by attaching entities—both the befuddled and the not so savory deceased. They glommed onto me and I had to be rescued from their clutches on a fairly regular basis. In the two and a half years since Duane's work, that has not happened once—a nightmarish condition I thought was a life sentence was finished! (I still do perceive such entities, and can help them if they are merely confused, but they do not attach to me in the suffocating way they once did.)

"As our work progressed, Duane began initiating me into the various dimensions, but I had a hard time letting him take me beyond the Fifth Dimension because I instantly felt I had found my spiritual home. I could feel the beings that lived there and loved them so much. Imagine finding a home peopled entirely by beings who are peaceful, loving, scholarly, talented, spiritually aware, highly evolved, and completely committed to service! I allowed Duane to go ahead with the initiations into Sixth and Seventh, reluctantly. On my own, however, I resolved to explore the Fifth Dimension, get to know the people, and to work my Buddhist behind off to be worthy of admission to that plane when this earth life is over. And in the time since Duane and I completed the work, I have formed bonds and working partnerships with several Fifth Dimension beings so that our joint efforts can bring knowledge of the light and its healing power to more of those on the plane who want to ascend. The artistic side of my nature that had never been developed is more and more a part of my life work, in part due to these partnerships.

"There have been a variety of other unforeseen effects of the series of Lightbody Activations. For instance, I am so much more telepathic now—maybe because my aura IS strong enough to allow me to open up more without being inundated. And my growth rate seems to have increased over-all, with a stronger commitment to working for the kind of inner peace I experienced in the Fifth Dimension. In short, my work with Duane has been an amazing catalyst, and I am so grateful for it."
D. C.

Testimonial from J. A.

"Duane Henkle is a powerful shaman, gifted healer, and a skilled Light worker. In addition, he is a deeply compassionate person. His work with the four activations is truly life changing, and often life transforming. The activations are the foundation for so much more, including psychic healing and past life work. Duane has the ability to see the core issue that needs to be healed and how to heal it—in order for his client to move on to ascension. I am someone who has benefited profoundly from his work." J. A.

Testimonial from B. C.

"My name is B. C. and I live in a small town in Iowa. I have had a lot of strange things happen to me all my life. Having dreams that are so real, seeing people that I know are dead, people/spirits I do not know coming to me. I thought I was going nuts!

"My first husband was killed when he was 35 years old and I was 33. Things really got bad then. Since then I have remarried to a wonderful understanding man. He has a friend who is an astrologer and she has helped me by explaining the strange things that were happening to me and telling me that I was a medium. I just could not believe this. Well, she had me get in touch with Duane. I had a session with Duane. He explained everything that I was going through. When he told me that I had a mission in this life, and that I was to help spirits cross over to the other side. The amazing thing was (remember Duane knows nothing about me) he told me that before returning to this life that I had accepted an assignment to help people or groups of people that were confused about how to cross over to the other side.

"He explained that I was a lighthouse in the night for these souls. Before I accepted the mission, I made a deal with Spirit that I was to have a partner that would understand my work, when it was time for me to start helping others get to the other side. My first husband would have put me in the LOONEY-BIN.

"My husband now understands it all and supports me in my assignment. Duane is an amazing man. I have learned a lot about myself and my mission in this life, all thanks to Duane and his ability to see and explain to me in a way that I could understand and feel comfortable with my mission.

I am still learning with the help of Duane, my Angels, Guides, my loving husband and family who believe and understand. Thank you and may God bless you."
B. C.

Testimonial from M. C.

"In my early sessions with Duane I experienced the 'reality' of the Lightbody Activations. His work took me into a higher dimension, and the consciousness of Oneness. After the sessions I found that I could go to that dimension quite easily. This transferred to my work as a Cranial Sacral Therapist. While working with my clients now, there is a moment when a 'switch' goes on and we (both my client and myself) are in the healing energy of the 5th, 6th and 7th dimensions. This is when the healing occurs.

"The clearing and past life work that Duane has done with me removed physical, emotional, mental and spiritual blockages. I could write a chapter on this, but simply will say that I now walk the planet lightly, more open to the energies, and with a deeper understanding of the Soul's journey toward ascension. I am truly grateful to Duane for the work he is doing in bringing Lightbody Activations to our planet."
M. C.

Testimonial from C. K. C.

(NOTE: This man lives in a European country and is a medical doctor. He is a student of ascension and is familiar with most of the activation methods available on the planet. He has activated many people using Duane Henkle's method. He considers Duane's method the easiest to do and the most powerful. This testimonial has been slightly edited for clarity, as English is not the good doctor's first language.)

"Many times I have wondered what would happen if I activated someone without telling the person about what I was doing. The objective here was to get genuine information about what the person would feel, hear and see. So I chose this child Lazandra, nine years old, my sister's daughter, my niece. I asked her to lie down on the table and just relax.

"When I was running the strands of light from the six chakras to the heart chakra, she said, 'I feel very hot in my heart.'

"When I was encasing and spinning the core of light in the spinal column, she said, 'My feet feel very hot. My hands feel warm. My spine is getting hot. I feel heavy.'

"When I was encasing and spinning the first and second cylinders of light, she said, 'I feel very heavy. My legs feel heavy, heavier than my entire body. I feel only my head. It is like I am only my head.'

"When I was encasing and spinning the last cylinder of light, activating the spiritual body, she said, 'I do not feel my body anymore. I feel I am flowing out of my body. I feel I am floating in the air.'

"I finished the activation process and waited about 15 minutes. Then I counted down from ten to one, and I woke up the child. Then I asked her to tell me what she saw, heard or felt. She said, 'I think I fell asleep and when I woke up, I was in a warm place, full of light, peace and love. I was lying down on a very comfortable bed. A beautiful lady came to me and told me, 'Welcome, my sweetie, this place will be your home in 2012.'

"When Lizandra told me these last words, she was crying tears of joy and her eyes were full of light. This child did not know about 2012. I never told her about 2012 before. So this information is true. She had been in the Fifth Dimension."
C. K. C

Bibliography

Bibliography

Arguelles, Jose, Ph.D. *The Mayan Factor – Path Beyond Technology,* Santa Fe NM: Bear & Company, 1987.

Baer, Randall N. and Vicki Vittitow Baer. *The Crystal Connection – A Guidebook for Personal and Planetary Ascension,* San Francisco CA: Harper & Row, 1987.

Baldwin, William J. *Spirit Releasement Therapy – A Technique Manual,* Terra Alta WV: Headline Books, Inc., 1992.

Beaconsfield, Hannah. *Welcome to Planet Earth — A Guide for Walk-ins and Starseeds,* Sedona, AZ, Light Technology Publications, 1997.

Berney, Charlotte. *Fundamentals of Hawaiian Mysticism,* Freedom CA: The Crossing Press, 2000.

Carroll, Lee. "The End Times (New Information for Personal Peace)," *Kryon Book I,* Del Mar, CA: The Kryon Writings, 1993.

Carroll, Lee. "Don't Think Like a Human! (Channeled Answers to Basic Questions)," *Kryon Book I,* Del Mar CA: The Kryon Writings, 1994.

Carroll, Lee. "Alchemy of The Human Spirit (A Guide to Human Transition into the New Age)," *Kryon Book I,* Del Mar CA: The Kryon Writings, 1995.

Carroll, Lee. "Partnering with God (Practical Information for the New Millennium)," *Kryon Book VI,* Del Mar CA: The Kryon Writings, 1997.

Carroll, Lee. "Letters from Home (Loving Messages from the Family)," *Kryon Book VI,* Del Mar CA: The Kryon Writings, 1999.

Carroll, Lee. *The New Beginning—Kryon Book Nine.* The Kryon Writings, Inc., 2002.

Carroll, Lee. *The New Dispensation—Kryon Book Ten.* The Kryon Writings, Inc., 2004.

Essene, Virginia and Sheldon Nidle. *You Are Becoming A Galactic Human,* Santa Clara CA: S.E.E. Publishing Company, 1994

Free, Wynn. *The Reincarnation of Edgar Cayce? – Interdimensional Communication & Global Transformation,* Berkeley, CA, Frog, Ltd. 2004

Harner, Michael. *The Way of the Shaman – A Guide to Power and Healing,* New York NY: Bantum Books, 1980.

Hawkins, David R., M.D., Ph.D., *Power vs. Force—The Hidden Determinants of Human Behavior,* Carlsbad, CA, Hay House, 2002.

Henkle, Duane and Stone, Diana. *The Lightbody Activation Manual.* Vancouver, WA, Crystal Triangle Publishing, 2002.

Hoagland, Richard. *The Monuments on Mars.* North Atlantic Press, 1990.

Ingerman, Sandra. *Soul Retrieval – Mending the Fragmented Self,* New York NY: Harper San Francisco, 1991.

Long, Max Freedom. *The Secret Science Behind Miracles,* Marina del Rey CA, DeVorss & Co., 1954.

Long, Max Freedom. *The Secret Science at Work – New Light on Prayer,* Marina del Rey CA: DeVorss & Co., 1953. (Now subtitled as: *The Huna Method as a Way of Life.)*

Lowary, Sheila Petersen. *The 5th Dimension – Channels to a New Reality,* New York, NY: Fireside Simon & Schuster, Inc. 1988.

Matthews, Caitlin. *Psychic Shield – A Personal Handbook of Psychic Protection,* Berkeley, CA, Ulysses Press, 2006.

Melchizedek, Drunvalo. *The Ancient Secret of the Flower of Life,* Vol. 1, Flagstaff AZ, Light Technology Publishing, 1998.

Melchizedek, Drunvalo. *The Ancient Secret of the Flower of Life,* Vol. 2, Flagstaff AZ: Light Technology Publishing, 2000.

Miller, David K. *Connecting with the Arcturians,* Pine AZ: Planetary Heart Publications, 1998.

Milanovich, Dr. Norma J. *We, The Arcturians (A True Experience),* Albuquerque NM: Athena Publishing, 1990.

Modi, Shakuntala, M.D. *Remarkable Healings – A Psychiatrist Discovers Unsuspected Roots of Mental and Physical Illness,* Charlottesville VA: Hampton Roads Publishing, 1997.

Myss, Caroline. *Sacred Contracts – Awakening Your Divine Potential,* New York, NY, Three Rivers Press, 2003.

Newton, Michael, Ph.D. *Journey of Souls – Case Studies of Life Between Lives,* St. Paul, MN, Llewellyn Publications, 1994.

Newton, Michael, Ph.D. *Life Between Lives – Hypnotherapy for Spiritual Regression,* St. Paul, MN, Llewellyn Publications, 2004.

Phylos, Orpheus and Virginia Essene. *Earth, the Cosmos and You – Revelations by Archangel Michael,* Santa Clara CA: S.E.E. Publishing Company, 1999.

Paddison, Sara, *The Hidden Power of the Heart,-- Achieving Balance and Fulfillment in a Stressful World, Boulder Creek, CA,* Planetary Publications, 1995.

Pila of Hawaii. *The Secrets and Mysteries of Hawaii.* Health Communications, 1995.

Roberts, Jane. *Seth Speaks: The Eternal Validity of the Soul.* Prentice-Hall, 1972.

Steinbrecher, Edwin C. *The Inner Guide Meditation,* York Beach ME: Samuel Weiser, Inc. 1988.

Stubbs, Tony. *An Ascension Handbook,* Lithia GA: New Leaf Distributing, 1999.

Tachi-ren, Tashira. *What Is Lightbody?,* Lithia GA: New Leaf Distributing, 1999.

Talbot, Michael. *The Holographic Universe,* New York NY: Harper Perennial, 1991.

Villoldo, Alberto, Ph.D. *Mending the Past and Healing the Future with Soul Retrieval.* Carlsbad, CA, Hay House, Inc., 2005.

Villoldo, Alberto, Ph.D., *Shaman, Healer, Sage,* New Your, NY, Harmony Books, 2000

Waya, Ai Gvhdi. *Soul Recovery and Extraction,* Cottonwood AZ: Blue Turtle Publishing, 1993.

Wilcock, David. URL: www.ascension2000.com

Wilcock, David. *The Shift of the Ages*. URL: http://www.ascension2000.com

Wilcock, David. *The Science of Oneness*. URL: http://www.ascension2000.com

Wilcock, David. *The Divine Cosmos*. URL: www.ascension.2000.com

Wing, R.L. *The I Ching Workbook.* Main Street Books, Doubleday, 1979.

Books and Crystal Triangle Training Videos For Sale

Plus

Shipping Information

SPECIAL OFFER!

Order from Our Secure Credit-Card Web Site!
www.dianastone.com or
e-mail Diana Stone at DianaS@SpiritOne.com

Both books One and Two of THE TECHNOLOGY OF ASCENSION SERIES are being offered on a special authors' discount sale.

Book One, *The Lightbody Activation Manual*, 3rd Ed., Duane Henkle and Diana Stone

On sale for $15.00 + S&H (Cover price $17.95)

(Quote from Book One, *The Lightbody Activation Manual)*:

A must read for the 21st Century Spiritual Seeker

The year A.D. 2012 marks the most significant in the history of Planet Earth: Our ascension into the Fifth Dimension. The lightbody is the vehicle that transports us into this new reality. You can't go home without it! The cosmic doorways are now open so that the lightbody may be activated by directly accessing the energies of the Fifth Dimension. Lightbody Activation now moves one giant step beyond meditations, mantras and affirmations.

Spirit called Duane Henkle to Hawaii where Pleiadian Beings revealed the secrets of Lightbody Activation using the power of the Crystal Triangle. Their prescribed pattern of movements includes three programmed crystals used by two individuals who work as partners to activate each other's energy fields. These nine easy steps take about 20 minutes per session.

Co-author Diana Stone (Duane's sister) conducted three years of field tests with a group of healers and metaphysicians in Northwestern United States. Read their comments about the power and simplicity of the Crystal Triangle used to activate the lightbody!

Read the special chapter on Crystal Triangle Healing! Learn how to do Crystal Triangle healing yourself! The material includes techniques for clearing past lives, releasing earthbound souls, activating DNA transformation and much more.

Read how to incorporate Crystal Triangle energy work into a professional practice.

GET EXTRA COPIES OF BOOK ONE or THIS BOOK!!

Book Two (this book), *The Ascension Guidebook*, Duane Henkle, (Cover price $17.95)

Individually On sale for $15.00 +S&H

Set of Book One plus Book Two for $27.00 total + S&H ($ 3.00 added savings)

Crystal Triangle Lightbody Activation Detailed Training Video!

(Available in either VCR tape or DVD format)

$45.00 plus shipping and handling

The Two Authors of *The Lightbody Activation Manual* Demonstrate the Nine-Step Method

Duane Henkle and Diana Stone demonstrate exactly how to do a Crystal Triangle Lightbody Activation. Each one of the nine-steps is shown on the VHS tape video or DVD and also includes additional information not found in the book. This two-hour instructional presentation is equally appropriate for practitioners to use for training groups at workshops, for individuals to share with friends in their homes or for one person working alone. See exactly what to do. The training film is used in conjunction with the book and does not replace it.

Contents include:

- **An explanatory Introduction by Diana Stone clarifying questions asked by readers**
- **A keynote lecture about ascension and lightbody by Diana Stone**
- **A step-by-step Lightbody Activation demonstrated by Duane Henkle**
- **A question and answer session with Duane Henkle**
- **Duane's special blessing to end an activation**

- **Duane leads someone doing her first activation**
- **How to program your crystals**
- **Which crystals to use for activations**
- **A question and answer period with Dr. Otha Wingo**
- **A demonstration of solo Crystal Triangle**
- **A demonstration of liquid light**
- **A demonstration of opening the third eye.**
- **Using Lightbody Activations with other healing modalities**

The above sale prices are only available from the authors. Order by phone (360-546-2497 with VISA or MC) or on the secure Web site www.DianaStone.com.

Prices subject to change without notice.

Shipping

BOOKS AND INSTRUCTION VIDEOS (VHS TAPES or DVDs)

Author discounted orders may be made on the secure ordering part of the Web site: www.dianastone.com.

All orders within continental United States are sent by Media Mail (6-9 days) only. Shipping and handling costs are $3.00 plus $0.50 per book, instructional tape or DVD in total order.
(e.g. 1 book plus 2 DVDs = 3 items total. Therefore, $3.00 + $1.50 = $4.50 total S&H)

Orders larger than 10 total items should be made directly with Crystal Triangle Publishing.

Book orders for shipment to foreign destinations should be made through Amazon.com or bookstores where available. Foreign **video** orders must be made by phone or e-mail to Crystal Triangle Publishing at dianas@spiritone.com.

Coming Soon!

THE TECHNOLOGY OF ASCENSION SERIES
Book Three

Countdown to Ascension

By
Diana Stone

Projected publication date: early 2007

Humanity's leap into the Fifth Dimension raises many questions about what we should do NOW! What happens after lightbody? How do we prepare for ascension? The Ascension Activations are tied to a process of clearing negative energies. This book deals with past life memories, entity invasion, traumatic emotional and physical trauma, toxic relationships and more. Removing these blocks releases you to greater creativity and service.

The Creative Intelligence operates through immutable universal laws. Access to personal guidance through these great forces may seem beyond all possibilities. Unfamiliar realities challenge and shock entrenched belief systems. Diana Stone climbs into the trenches of Third Dimension consciousness to act as your guide.

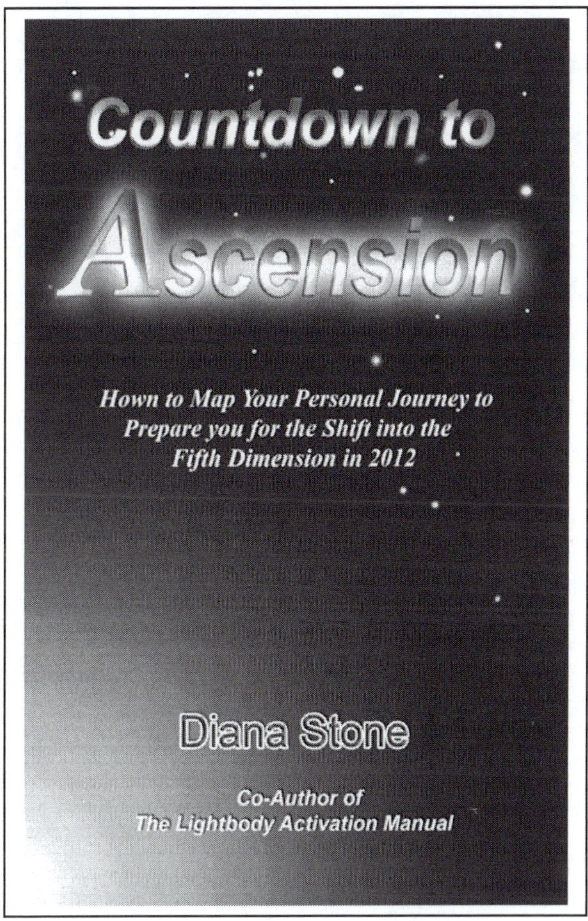

Through her own personal journey from Harmonic Concordance November 8, 2003 to the Mayan Calendar Breakthrough Celebration May 27-28, 2006, readers will experience how the universe whispers in their ears.

Through author Stone's free e-mail newsletters, readers rode the roller coaster through the scary valleys of consciousness, split their sides at the hilarious antics of the Trickster archetype and confronted startling new concepts and rules for the grand Game of Life. Letters from readers just like you confirmed that although the Game is sometimes almost unbearably challenging, you are not crazy or alone.

It is gritty. It is real. It is spittle, hair, blood and bone. Diana's Stone's delightful wit and earthy crone wisdom is pure magic.

Refer to Diana Stone's Web site at www.dianastone.com for continuing updates about publication dates and to subscribe to Diana's FREE Newsletter. Contact her in Vancouver, Washington. by phone at 360-546-2497 or e-mail DianaS@SpiritOne.com.